WATERCOLOR

... A CHALLENGE

Mountain Landscape

WATERCOLOR

... A CHALLENGE

by Leonard Brooks

REINHOLD PUBLISHING CORPORATION

New York

To Reva

ACKNOWLEDGMENT

The author wishes to thank the galleries and private collectors who have allowed the reproduction of his paintings from their collections. Also to express his gratitude to Charles Allen Smart and Earle Birney for their advice and encouragement, as well as to the many artists who have helped with their criticism and counsel.

CONTENTS

"The only thing is to see. Oh doubtless a mediocre man copying nature will never produce a work of art because he really looks without seeing, and though he may have noted each detail minutely, the result will be flat and without character. But the profession of the artist is not meant for the mediocre, and to them the best counsels will never succeed in giving talent. The artist, on the other hand, sees; that is—his eye, grafted on his heart, reads deeply into the bosom of nature. That is why the artist has only to trust to his eyes."

RODIN
Artists on Art
Pantheon Books Inc.

INTRODUCTION

Painting watercolors can be fun. It can also be one of the most exasperating and disappointing occupations known to man. Like trout-fishing, or golf, it has its relative degrees of skill; its very difficulties offer a challenge which keeps us, amateurs and professionals alike, fascinated and absorbed in the art.

It is many years since, as a boy in my teens, I sat, shivering but exultant, before a landscape, trying to paint my first watercolor out-of-doors. It was Christmas day and the snow was deep on the ground. A kind uncle had presented me with a small, tin paint-box and brush, and unwittingly, a life-time career.

I remember slipping away that afternoon from the festivities around the Christmas tree to the willow-lined creek behind the house. I worked on a borrowed writing pad, scrubbing at the tiny, hard cakes of color, trying to put down the heavy, gray sky, the orange and scarlet willow branches fringing the bank. Somehow I caught some of it on paper and ran back to the house thrilled—and chilled to the bone.

It was not until I reached the warmth of the room that I noticed that the still wet washes had partially crystallized and frozen. I watched in horror as my masterpiece melted and dissolved, the colors running in odd pat-

terns into each other. The reds and blacks softened, creeping across the sky in arabesques of fine branches.

Entranced I watched the watercolor make a new life of its own. By some magic the mood of that winter day spread its charm on the hard niggling washes I had painted.

It looked good! Without mentioning the fact that my picture had practically painted itself, I presented my work of art proudly to my uncle. His words were like music in my ears.

"My! That really feels like winter!"

I have never forgotten that day. It was a long time before my colors earned praise like that again. But I had learned an important lesson. It is not altogether true that, as someone once said, "A watercolor is a series of accidents happening in the right place," but there is some truth in the statement. If you find out what the watercolor wants to do, you at least stand some chance of making it obey *your* control.

Another book on watercolor? Yes, I believe there is a need for a book which will help the amateur and student to move ahead to a higher creative level than that aimed for in most "how-to-do-it" manuals; too many of these books for beginners play down to a standard far below the intelligence and creative potentialities of the part-time painter. Today, when many thousands of men and women are devoting time and thought to the joys and tribulations of the paintbrush, the superficial trick and easy short cut are losing out. Professionals in their own fields, who are amateurs painting for pleasure, know only too well that the rich satisfactions of painting do not come in "easy lessons" or with numbered reproductions to copy.

In these pages I have tried to bridge the gap between the purely technical and elementary approaches with some of the thinking processes which are at the foundation of all creative and imaginative art. Both new and traditional methods in the use of watercolor and casein are discussed and demonstrated, but always with the strong admonition that the technique is only part of a larger vocabulary which the painter must use in his own way. *How* and *what* he wishes to paint must inevitably be his decision alone.

Nevertheless, there are many general ideas which, if digested and used, can stimulate a personal interpretation. These are closely allied to the *way* the painter uses his techniques and are as useful as the knowledge of how to neutralize a primary color, or foreshorten a bending figure. Some of these ideas have been included in the text, though to do so has

been for me akin to walking a tightrope. The dangers of falling either to the side of aesthetic theory, or to a false underlining of "rules and recipes" are evident.

I have also preferred to use my own paintings throughout for demonstrations, not to show how it should be done, but because I have felt that I know and can explain my own children—with all their weaknesses—better than the offspring of others.

To the enthusiast—amateur and hardworking student—this book is addressed. Its justification will be their progress to better seeing and painting, and a clearer understanding of some of the problems which they, and all of us face, when we set out to paint.

San Miguel de Allende,
Mexico

THE IMPORTANCE OF DRAWING

Not being able to draw well is one of the many frustrations which plague the amateur, contributing to his lack of confidence and holding him back from progressing. Even when he has advanced beyond those early days when he self-consciously stated that he couldn't draw a straight line with a ruler, and knows that the "straight" line is the last thing in the world he needs to think about, he is still often irked and bothered by his lack of skill in draftsmanship.

Drawing is essential to any kind of successful painting in any media, but it need not be the bogey which many sensitive and talented beginners consider it to be. The *real* desire to paint will bring with it enthusiasm and patience. The time and energy needed to obtain a basic understanding of the principles of structural drawing, and to train the eye and hand to work together in easy rapport, will not be resented nor considered a chore by the true enthusiast. I have seldom found a student who has not been able, with serious application, to master the elementary mechanics of drawing within a matter of a few months.

Of course, such drawing is not the fluid, experienced line of the master draftsman, God-given and instinctive. Drawing, as we speak of it here, is the means of putting down with some degree of accuracy, relative proportions, outlines, and masses of chosen subjects; to understand how to make an object sit on a table, or appear to hang in the air if need be. It means too, the ability to make a road go up or down a hill when required, to draw an arch or cylinder without trouble, or to suggest the human figure.

Expressive drawing—the ability to make a line come to life, sensitive, heavy, vibrant or shrill—is of a more subtle order. So is the development of a sense of form, of the free, all-embracing scrawl which can capture a moment or mood on a scrap of paper by seizing the essentials and putting them down in a personal and lively notation.

You will be told at times by some teachers that an understanding of "mechanical" drawing is nonsense, that you need not bother yourself with any such cramping concerns. Look at the way children draw; do they bother about such things as proportion? Look at the latest style in current New York art exhibitions, and then think of the years you will save yourself by not having to spend time learning those mundane matters of perspective and proportions! Just go ahead and express yourself—did those successful primitive painters have to learn these things?

Lack of knowledge, inexperience, a false

conception of what the artist's job as a creative person really is, can be responsible for wasting much valuable time and paint. There is no doubt whatsoever that a basic understanding of essential techniques will be of the utmost help to the truly creative person in the expression of his feelings and ideas.

Most professionals, especially the more advanced and liberated ones, get this basic training early so that they can absorb it, utilize it, and if necessary forget about it as they go on to paint things in their personal, unique manner. Almost all painters assimilate the traditional crafts and skills at the beginning of their careers, and can call on this knowledge at any time. It is easy to see that the great contemporary painters are master technicians who have submitted themselves to the disciplines of rational training. Look at the magnificent drawing in Picasso's animal and bird etchings, the elaborate, sensitive studies in Braque's "Intimate Sketchbook," recently published. Have you felt surprised at times when you've seen the splendid studies and pen drawings of figures and landscape by artists noted for their non-objective and experimental paintings?

For the painter in watercolor, ability to draw is a major necessity. Practical considerations make it imperative that he be able to put down cleanly and decisively the framework of his subject. He must not rub and scrub at his paper. Everything he puts down shows, from the first line to the last brushstroke. There is no chance to camouflage nor to cover over weak passages. The technique itself demands skill with the brush, for a clean deft handling will always win out over a harried, hesitant and weak delineation.

This ability can only come with practice and concentrated hard work. Throughout this book I will reiterate the necessity of constant drawing, both as a compositional training and as a discipline to eventually paint watercolors of real merit. Give yourself a number of hours daily devoted to some kind of drawing. Fill your sketchbooks with notes and studies. You will never regret doing so.

There are many fine books which will help you. One of the best, "The Natural Way to Draw," by Nicolaïdes, sets out a system of study which, if followed faithfully will develop your abilities in all the essentials of fine draftsmanship. The real pleasure in painting will only come when you have surmounted the essential vocabulary and craft. These pleasures are dividends returned to you after you can afford to concentrate on the excitement of genuine interpretation without too much concern for the mechanics.

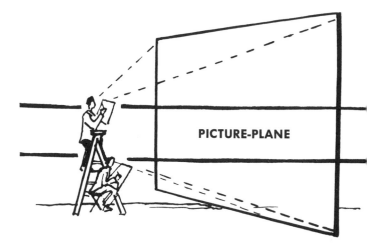

PICTURE-PLANE

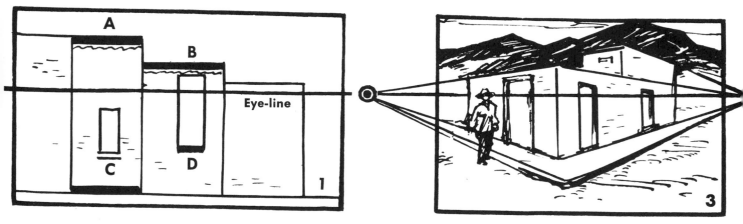

A

B

Eye-line

C

D

1

A

B

C

D

3

THE OPTICAL ILLUSION

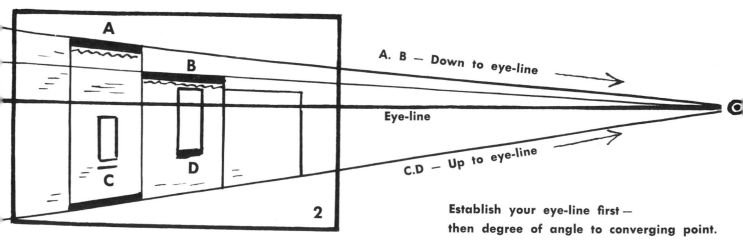

A

B

Eye-line

C

D

2

A. B — Down to eye-line

C.D — Up to eye-line

Establish your eye-line first —
then degree of angle to converging point.

Certainly you will be able to paint pictures without knowing anything about scientific perspective. The Chinese and Persian painters did centuries ago and some of them still do. It was not until the fifteenth century that the artist took the theories of the scientists of the early Renaissance and brought the mechanical art of the optical illusion to its highest creative levels. The discoveries, which enabled the Giants of painting such as Leonardo da Vinci to paint masterpieces incorporating exact and detailed realism, have changed little today.

What has changed is the necessity for the artist of today to use these geometrical laws. In later pages of this book I have pointed out how visual realism has become less and less the desire of the contemporary creative painter, and how he has become more concerned with the expressive control of his areas and forms in "pictorial space"—a somewhat different task than the correct projection of visual fact rendered according to the strict mathematics of perspective.

Away from the draftingboard of the architect, or the confines of an advertising drawing, the artist may reach his finest personal interpretation without paying attention to the laws of converging lines, or purposely disregarding what he does know. On the other hand, he may call upon these laws to help him understand the structure of his subject matter, or subdue and modify their workings to his will. An understanding of the useful and rudimentary laws of perspective is not too difficult to acquire and most artists explore its theories early in their studies.

One method of seeing how perspective can be used in an expressive and imaginative way is to collect examples of work by well-known men which use the mechanics of receding form in a creative personal manner, far removed from literal copying. Look up the "Perspective of a City" or the studio drawings of Paul Klee; study the creations of the great interpreter of perspective—Piranesi and his "Prisons"; observe the work of modern men such as Ben Shahn who use or break the rules of perspective in a lively and convincing manner. You can even learn from the covers of the New Yorker magazine at times when they use the consciously-naive designs which are painted in a pseudo-primitive and charming manner.

Most adults today can remember watching a teacher in elementary school disentangling himself from bits of string, assorted cubes and plinths and imaginary vanishing points, with which he demonstrated the wonders of converging parallel lines. Even a telephone doodler can make a fair representation of a box or cube lying on the flat paper. Yet, it is surprising how befuddled the same doodler can get when he takes up painting and is accosted with the problem of representing a slightly more complex variation of the same box. I am constantly meeting students—even art school graduates—who find themselves embarrassed when they face a down-hill road and wish to represent it in their pictures in a realistic way. It is so easy too, to write off the uphill slope which insists on looking as if it is going downhill as "expressive distortion," or to tell oneself that knowing the underlying theories of the optical illusion may inhibit the creative capacity.

Generally, too much awareness of perspective will stiffen up your sketches. Artists with an over-thorough background of mechanical techniques find it difficult to break away from the tyranny of exactitude. Their work has often the appearance of an architectural rendering. On the other hand, however, some understanding of "artist's perspective" is essential if you are going to work with visual forms from nature.

On the following pages I have included a simple explanation of the fundamental propositions of basic perspective you'll find useful.

Drawing No. 1 shows the object (in this case the front of a wall) flat to—or parallel with—the surface of your picture when you hold it up to your eye level. If you imagine the paper as a piece of glass you are looking through, it will help you. Where your eye strikes the center of the glass we imagine a line to be stretched parallel with the top and bottom of your glass or paper. This we will call the eye line. This line moves up and down with you when you climb a stepladder or sit

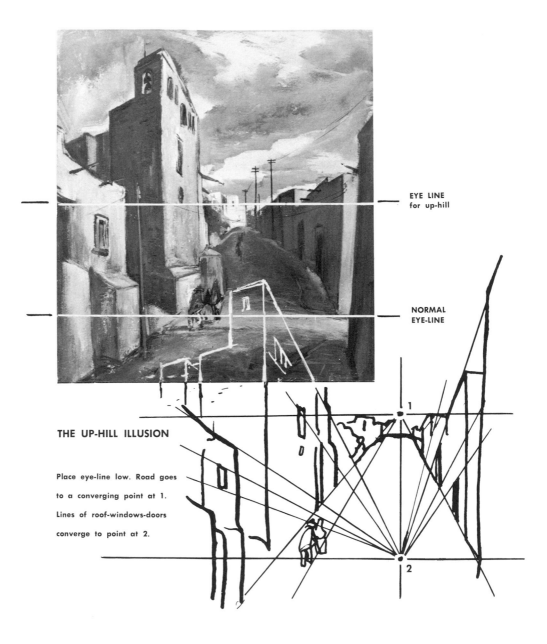

EYE LINE
for up-hill

NORMAL
EYE-LINE

THE UP-HILL ILLUSION

Place eye-line low. Road goes
to a converging point at 1.
Lines of roof-windows-doors
converge to point at 2.

down. This is also the horizon line you observe when you look out to sea.

As soon as you turn the wall of the house
at an angle to the surface of the glass, the
fun begins and you have the perspective
theory in a nutshell. Notice how the lines
above the eye line appear to go *down,* and
how the lines *below* the eye line appear to go
up, both heading for a common meeting place
on your eye line. If you change the angle of
your wall the meeting place moves along the
eye line. It is possible to have many of these
converging points in one picture if you have
many different angles to your picture surface. Some will be to the left, some to the
right, even outside the picture surface altogether—but always on the eye line. But notice
that we are only talking about *parallel horizontal lines.* This is very important to remember for as soon as they are not, and are
sloping or inclined lines such as the open lid
of a box or book, they will have converging
lines going to a point somewhere above or below the eye line. The paintings with the per-

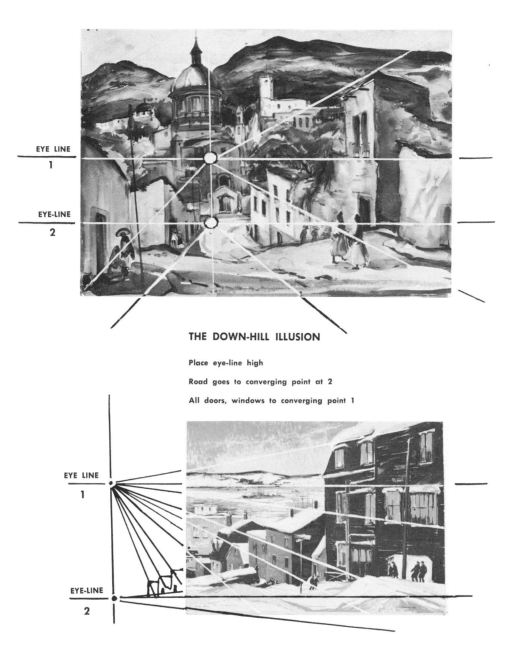

EYE LINE
1

EYE-LINE
2

THE DOWN-HILL ILLUSION

Place eye-line high

Road goes to converging point at 2

All doors, windows to converging point 1

EYE LINE
1

EYE-LINE
2

spective lines drawn over them illustrate how there are then *two* eye lines with their converging points.

Most of the variations of perspective problems you meet in ordinary sketching will stem from these propositions. It is seldom that you will see a house as basic as that shown in No. 3, but if you remember that geometric solids such as the cube, cone and cylinder are the basis of most objects you will soon be able to sort out more complex forms. Once you have mastered the principle of receding par-allel lines your own reasoning and observation will enable you to call upon perspective when you wish.

Add to this some study of the cylinder and circle in perspective, and you will have no fear of the mechanics of drawing when you wish to create an optical illusion.

Several fine books on the subject are listed in the appendix. The University of California Press volume by Joseph William Hull is excellent for the art student, as well as Ernest Watson's book on "Creative Perspective."

THE EXPLORATIVE LINE

A corner of the studio with jugs and bowls set out for painting. You will find it good training in drawing to develop an "eloquent line." There was no desire here to do a mechanical drawing and there was no blocking out of accurate perspective lines or literal transcription.

I like to think of this line as an "inventorial" or "explorative" line. Start anywhere on the page and draw slowly as your eye follows the contours and forms. Don't take the pen off the paper more than necessary. An even, slow line of this type will have its own character. You are concerned with a mental assessment of natural appearances. Use an ordinary writing nib on a smooth drawing paper. Gray washes were touched in lightly, and here and there lines were drawn on the paper while damp to allow the ink line to soften and run.

Study the pen drawings of Matisse if you would see a master's use of exquisite contour drawing, but don't let the simplicity fool you. Matisse made thousands of drawings to achieve such rare command over line.

One Ring Circus

MODELS ARE FREE

Thin line, thick line, pencil, pen; any way you choose, but get it down on paper.

For many years now I have made it a habit to jot down in a small book, quick notes of figures, animals, or combinations of both which would be useful whenever I need to put a figure in my watercolors painted in the studio. A reference to this book enables me to find an authentic figure when I require one, or suggests others taken "from life."

The selection of some of the notes shown here were done while waiting for a train, waiting for the rain to stop, or sitting in the middle of nowhere when the car broke down.

It is important to collect pages of this kind. When you first start doing so, do not be ashamed of your first scrawls, and do not expect to get a finished or satisfactory drawing every time.

Try and see the whole gesture of movement, fix the image in your mind first, and then put it down in one piece. A few lines well-chosen can fix a pose for you and you can elaborate on it later. Think of your sketching as a kind of writing, using the pen to say something about the movement or mood of people. They may be standing, sitting or walking—look for the lines which will make this clear.

There are many fine books on figure drawing. The Nicolaïdes volume mentioned previously is one of the best to help you begin figure drawing from life. A session in a life class, plus some hours in the fundamentals of simple anatomy, will give you confidence. The ability to add figures to your work is a gratifying addition to your skills.

The circus painting on the previous page was made from quick notes of this kind. Further data on the casein technique used is on Page 145.

1. Spot out a few strong darks *trying to see the whole composition on the paper* before you begin. *Pick out important accents, emphasize shadow forms to give a sense of solidity. Train hand and eye to work together.*

SUBJECTS ARE EVERYWHERE

2. *A quick jotting down of this kind should give you the skeleton of your picture, the structural bones on which you will build your color, textures, and if you must have them, all the details. The use of the white paper in this sketch practically demands that a watercolor be done from it.*

By taking the felt nib out of the pen and using it flat on the paper like a piece of crayon, you can make broad, brush-like tones with it, which I prefer to using the broad-edged nibs supplied with the pens.

3. *Interesting combinations of forms are everywhere, often where you least expect them. This was drawn on a scrap of paper from a San Francisco apartment window. It was the basis for several paintings done later. Even the back of an envelope will do to draw on when something moves you to paint it. Get some of it down. Once you have formed the habit of constantly sketching, you will find even a hint or two will help to refresh your memory.*

4. *Another quick one. Enough data in this to paint up. The strong forms of light and dark on the trees, the suggestion of dark sky and late afternoon light brings this moment back vividly to me. Brightly colored boats and water textures. Can you visualize a color scheme for this sketch? Why not try it for an exercise?*

THE ARTIST'S EYE

Having made up our minds that drawing will be the thing which we will be constantly practising, and that it will inevitably get better in proportion to the number of pages we cover, we are ready to enter the wonderful and complicated world of composing. Composition—the selection and conception of our material for picture making—is the kernel of our art. Without it, our techniques, even an outstanding facility to draw, are entirely meaningless.

How do we select, from the mass of detail and countless forms about us, the significant lines and shapes which will be the basis of our sketch? How can we learn to ignore color, and irrelevant detail, while we search out the essential basic structure on which lesser details are built?

To be able to do so, we must cultivate the "artist's eye," a far different eye than we are accustomed to using in our every day practical comings and goings. What may appeal to us as ordinary onlookers—"How lovely that mass of flowers looks in the field!" —may not be of much value to us here. We are limited in many ways, and if we understand some of these limitations we will stand a chance of working within their bounds. How many times will the artist hear from well-meaning friends: "Have you been up on

Felt-pen sketchbook techniques

Trim nibs with razor blade

Chisel point

Snake Point? Magnificent, you can see for miles, a remarkable sight. You should go up there and paint it sometime."

We know beforehand that it will probably be a futile trip. It may be a panorama most pleasing to the general eye, but dull, flat, useless for picture-making when we think of it in terms of a number of lines and masses on our paper or canvas.

We are wise to give ourselves a chance with the type of subject which appeals to us most strongly. This is not to say that there are only certain themes suitable for picture-making. The artist's job is to seek out and find with fresh vision all kinds of subject which we would, as casual onlookers, never think worthy of a creative effort. The artist may come along and make a masterpicce of the thing which thousands pass by every day. And always we must remember the qualities and possibilities of our medium; there are many subjects which lend themselves better to our media—in this case watercolor—than others. A violinist, or the composer who writes for him, would never try to produce a symphonic overture from the violin alone.

Any medium we choose as our means of expression has its own inherent qualities, which should be exploited to the utmost. What some of the particular qualities of watercolor are, will be discussed later on in this book.

As painters, we have long since stopped vying with the camera eye with its mechanical mastery of fact and detail. Photography has made our problem and the direction we must go much clearer for us. Even so, the tradition of the artist drawing "what he sees" is often misunderstood. Rodin's words (Page 9) clearly define the difference between copying and "seeing with the eyes and heart."

Today we are going to concentrate on cultivating this "artist's eye." We'll need only our sketchbook and felt-nib pen and the zest to fill some of the pages. What shall we choose to begin with?

Pick anything which appeals to you, but make sure it has big elements, strong shapes, a variety of light and dark tones to help you simplify. Look for one dominant note and lesser notes to augment it. Has our subject a basic design form which caught our eye in the first place as we looked about? Perhaps it is based on a series of curved forms, those tree boughs rolling across the rhythms of the majestic cumulus clouds. Or is it attractive to us because it is formed from a number of horizontal lines repeating themselves into infinity on the horizon? What is the *essential* visual structure which attracts us?

If we can feel this underlying design beneath the myriad details obscuring it, we are in the first stake of composing. One way to help ourselves pin down the essence of our composition is to make a number of small scribbles approximately three inches wide,

cessful composition, and it must be there when you are finished with your more detailed study, hidden though it may seem to be. This is the secret of carrying out a satisfying conclusion to your work, and where most amateurs go astray. They lose the kernel, the heart of the subject in details, changes of mind and the lesser concerns of color-mixing and technical procedures.

Good color, texture, drawing, fine subject—all of these will not redeem a badly conceived arrangement of lines and masses on the flat surface of our paper.

On Pages 24-28 are shown some of these rapid notes as torn out of my sketchbooks. Drawing them in a box is important as it defines the edges of your composition to which you must relate the main lines and forms of your drawing. Remember that in composition a line by itself means nothing. Its existence begins when it is placed in relation to the corners and edges of its frame.

Work freely, remembering that you are not trying to produce a finished presentable sketch. Your purpose is to collect information, to select what you want, minimizing or emphasizing as you wish. With a good morning's work you should collect three or four ideas and even have time to draw one of them up to a larger size in your sketchbook.

making sure we use the same proportion as the larger page we will fill later. In this way we can put down the germ of our sketch, trying many variations until we find one which seems to satisfy us the most. When you have found this one, ask yourself why you prefer this particular one. There will be some reason why it works visually, appeals more than the others. By analyzing all of the sketches you may find the answer. When you do, hang on to it through all the steps to come. It will be the structural framework, the key to the suc-

Here is a photograph of a subject waiting for your analysis. As it is, the composition does not work too well, the foreground seems unrelated, the boat badly placed. Try selecting from it, changing the proportions of the picture-plane, spotting out the accents in various positions. Small drawings of this kind will provide you with a choice before you begin your larger sketch. Don't be concerned with the drawing of detail, only the placing and break-up of your subject matter into the most attractive composition.

When you have decided which one you prefer, draw it up larger and use it as an exercise similar to those shown on Page 83 using one-color wash only.

DEVELOP YOUR SENSE
OF BASIC FORMS

1. *A photograph of the subject. For your first compositional experiments choose strongly lighted patterns, straightforward elements. A tree, a street and a few houses will serve.*

2. *A quick line analysis made in the sketch-book. Detail, accuracy of fact and tonal considerations have been disregarded in favor of sorting out a large, open pattern of well-defined areas. Remember you are not a camera, or competing with one.*

6. *A drawing done with more concern for the design of the subject as a watercolor. Here we have broken up the space in a more interesting fashion. The watercolor handling has dictated a looser rendering. The natural forms have been used to give a livelier impact of light and dark areas.*

5. *Here is what happens when you try to see too much and to record with photographic seeing alone. Although the light areas have been changed somewhat, there is too much intrusion of busy detail.*

3. If you isolate the elements of your subject, separating them in the manner shown here, you reduce the complications of accidental lighting on forms to their basic essentials. Using the geometric solids of sphere, cylinder, cube and cone will give your work a strong sense of solidity.

4. A freer construction keeping the large forms in mind. Plan out the big tonal patterns now without too much concern for precise light and shadow. Make your white and dark areas work towards a satisfying picture. On this foundation add details later, but keep the larger conception.

7 and 8. The use of geometric solids is shown in the reproduction of the winter sketch. The pen drawing shows the basic forms on which the enriched tonal scheme was planned. This basic, simple pattern holds together the structure and design of the many varied tones of black and white.

FIND YOUR OWN SYMBOLS

Perhaps you have, like so many others, found yourself coming to a full stop after the first exciting enthusiasm of splashing on water and pigment. You have reached a frustrating impasse which prevents you from progressing in your work. If you have, it is not unusual, for this happens to the best of us. The important thing is to find the cause and remedy for the bogged-down feeling.

The chances are that you have lost sight of the true impetus which set you to daubing at paper in the first place. It has become lost in the concern about the technique and handling of a difficult medium which can turn recalcitrant and sour, even when the spirit isn't flagging.

One of the best cures for this state of affairs is to go back to the beginnings, rediscover the urge to make marks and signs and symbols of the things we know and think about. Drawing was, in the first instance—some three hundred centuries ago—a thing of "magic." The hunter drew the antelope in his caves, a magic symbol painted for plenty, part of a primitive religious rite. Later this art became a thing of communication and record, but still a thing of religion and magic.

This urge to put down writings (have you

ever seen a child who was at a loss when you handed him a crayon?) is an instinctive one which all of us have, however atrophied it may become. It is, in some ways, as natural for us to want to draw as it is to make noises with our tongue.

This does not mean that we can return to the primitive simplicities—modern life has become too complex for that—nor can we see with the eyes of a child. What we *can* do, however, is to encourage some of our latent capacities to emerge from their deep and subconscious depths. As artists, even as beginners, we have already begun to do so. We are learning to see all over again, and to feel more vividly, sensations which will bring us closer to the "magic" which is art. ("And art is still magic or it is nothing, since it transforms us while revealing to us the spirit of the artist." Alan Houghton Brodrick in *Prehistoric Painting*.)

But how, you ask, is this done? One way which I have found useful in refreshing the springs of inspiration is to look back over the work of other less hurried times, from the early pre-historic cave-drawings to the Mayan cultures; to study the drawings of the old masters, particularly in their renderings of landscape. Here are worlds of magnificent

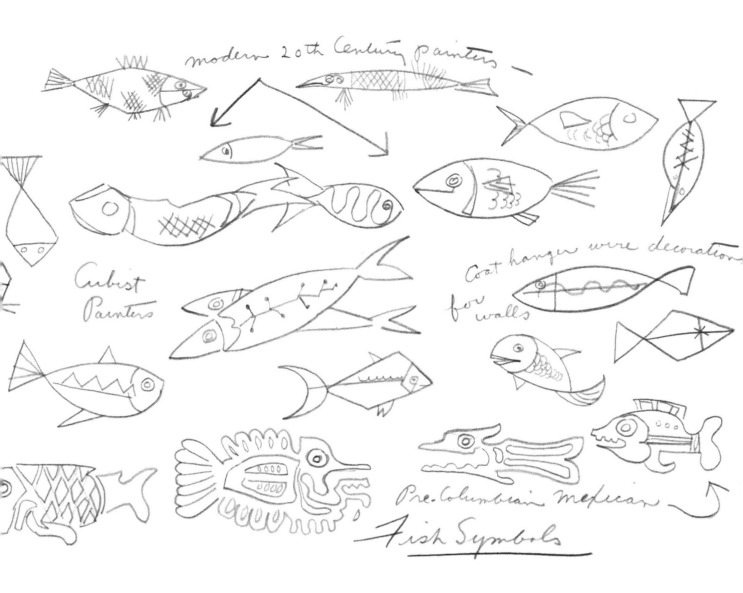

Modern 20th Century painters —

Cubist Painters

Coat hanger wire decorations for walls

Pre-Columbian Mexican

Fish Symbols

invention drawn from the natural life about them, which, in essence, was not so very much different from our own.

In the reproduction shown above, we have gathered a number of line drawings of fishes. Observe how the artists, from pre-Columbian days until now, have extracted vital forms and symbols from such simple material. Compare these inventions with the dull commercial rendering of a salmon on a tin of fish, or with a photograph of a fish, and you will realize what imagination, vitality, and a sense of magic can do. This is creative art. The "fishiness" of these fishes cannot be denied, even without coloring or photographic realism of form.

So shake yourself free from dullness and search out *your* symbols from *your* world. Renew your interest and refresh your vision with pencil and paper. In the next lesson we'll set out together to study other symbols, traditional and new.

SOME DECORATIVE ELEMENTS

We'll need the sketchbook, a bottle of ink and a small pointed sable brush for today's work. We are going to explore some of the traditional ways of making symbols and decorative designs from the material nature puts before us.

If we were Oriental artists working in the old, established culture, our task would be simple. I would merely hand you the scroll or notebooks of "The Eight Laws of Ledges for Painting Mountains, Rocks and Cliffs," or "The Twelve Laws of Dots for Painting Near or Distant Trees and Shrubs," and you could busy yourself memorizing them. Eventually "The Eighteen Laws for Painting the Lines of the Garment" would follow, and so on, until you had, over the years of study, established yourself as a sensitive reinterpretor of the set and accepted symbols. There would even be certain times of the year when you could or could not (if you were a self-respecting Poet of the Brush) paint certain subjects and seasons.

All of this would make it much easier for a teacher, who today would be branded as a stuffy, old reactionary for inhibiting the talents of the student, if he thought of such a thing.

Anyway, here are some of the accepted ways of using the brush to express some of the natural forms in landscape. Every time you paint from nature, using watercolor, you will be faced with the problem of selecting brush strokes, dots, lines and masses, and good luck to you if you can find or invent new ways every time.

It may help you to find your own symbols if you keep in mind some of the basic laws of design. These are as fundamental and inexorable as that our lungs breathe rhythmically and in time sequence, or our pulse beats in our wrist. To understand these laws, or better still, to feel them at the end of your brush, will give your work veracity and power.

One of the most valuable of these laws is that of repetition. It is in evidence everywhere as a human expression, from the repeated line or dot on our suit materials, wallpapers and ties, to the borders of concentric circles on a formal dinner plate. The symmetrical repeat so beloved by the primitive mind—the dot, dot, dash, dot, dot—like the beating of an African drum, is an elementary design form easily made visual in its repeat form; (. . — . .)

Then we must consider the more complicated forms of repetition, the variety of nonsymmetrical pattern. They indicate a more sophisticated expression calling forth our sense of balance and selection to a higher degree. The involved rhythms of a tree's branching system, the convolutions of a flower blossom, the grace of the human figure —all of these obey immutable mathematical laws of relative proportions and sequence.

Contrast, harmony, unity, flow and ebb, movement and quiet—all of these, which provide for us pleasurable visual reactions or disturb us by their lack, are necessarily part of the means with which we express ourselves. As artists, we soon learn to look to Nature as the source and foundation on which we build our own personal expression.

Lines too must be considered—their type, their visual effect on us. There are lines which move and spring, or crawl or lie calm; (see page 48) jagged lines of the diagonal and vertical like mountain forms or lightning. There are flowing lines and lines which start to take us on a path only to stop and fall in-

HORIZONTAL AND FLOWING

JAGGED AND VERTICAL

SPIRAL AND GROWTH

REPETITIONS

DOTS AND DASHES

COMBINATIONS

RHYTHMIC AND MOVING

terrupted, or change to rolling curves. Use these lines, experimenting with each type to see what they can do for you. Invent mountain forms repeating the type of line you are using, within itself, down to the smallest detail. Look about you as you walk through the park or garden. How many line forms will be suggested by a tree alone? Make foliage patterns using dots and squiggles, using the same form, yet repeating them in different order of size and groupings. Nets, shells and tiled roofs, rock piles and wharf pilings. If you fill several pages today, you will have learned two "musts" essential to the watercolor painter—more control of the brush, and the all-important art of inventing the decorative symbol from the vast and chaotic storehouse of nature.

WINDOW STILL LIFE

A free calligraphic sketch derived from natural forms—plants and potted flowers.

Pen line with ink drawn into wet paper to obtain soft, broken line. Photographic accuracy is sacrificed here to the excitement of line repetitions and patterns.

Direct and spontaneous sketches of this kind will help free you from the tyranny of slavish imitation. The subject here becomes unimportant. In the break-up of surface pattern, the lines themselves carry their own interest far beyond the interest of the objects themselves.

The color reproduction of "Easter Table" (opposite page) makes full use of repetitional forms, chairs, dishes and green veranda palings. Painted in casein from the embryo sketch shown on Page 57.

SOME CONTEMPORARY FORMS

I'm sure it won't take a second for you to recognize the page of drawings opposite. You may already have said, "Now that's more like it!" or "Oh, that modern stuff again."

There is no doubt that these forms are twentieth century and of this day. Fifty years ago they may have looked startling, but not any more. We have seen them, whether we want to or not, reproduced a million times in some form or other in every art magazine we pick up, and their influences are evident every time we get in and out of our latest model car. These forms have been used and abused to the extent of becoming cliches or material for "New Yorker" cartoons.

These forms sprang from the experiments and inventions of the postimpressionists. In their research into space-filling, in seeking new relationships of form and line, in finding more expressive means, their work was a bombshell which exploded in the face of a quieter, more romantic school who were busy finding out the mysteries of painting broken colors to express light and the moods of nature. Picasso's use of primitive imagery, derived from African sculpture, added a savage revaluation of expressive means. Based on the discoveries of Cezanne, he and his friends, under the banner of "cubists," sparked a whole generation of painters into seeking for "significant form".

Geometrical and nonobjective paintings followed fast, using purely design shapes and nonvisual subject matter. Picture making was to be unemotional, controlled, formal, and to deal only with the impersonal expression in plastic terms. This was the age of science, of vast new concepts of space and time, and, these painters argued, there must be a rule to "correct and curb each emotion." (Georges Braque) Out went the clutter of sentimental paintings and ridiculously over-decorated, rococo drawing rooms. Form and function became the cry and the clean lines of streamlined furniture and utilitarian objects came gradually to be accepted by civilization, almost as a necessity.

All of this is history now, written in countless volumes. We have become conditioned to these new forms as we find them now in our everyday life, almost as taken-for-granted accomplishments. Even if we knew "nothing about art" we would resent having delivered to us a 1920 radio cabinet or refrigerator model, even if it functioned as well as this year's latest design.

The danger, of course, for the student-painter today, is in aping, without understanding, the outward manifestations of stylizations and mannerisms which assail him from every side. A casual imitation is a far different thing from the genuine search for a deeper significance of reality which will demand perhaps a new form — far removed from a factual visual interpretation.

To understand the work of the contemporary masters, to be influenced by them and then to go on from there, adding more than superficial echoes of solutions already solved, takes courage and personal conviction of the highest order. To do this, to move forward rather than backward, is a task which has driven many a student to despair. It was one of them—a young man of talent and integrity who said, with insight—"Picasso has opened many new rooms for us, but many without doors to get out again."

For all of us—modern, academic, or somewhere in between—it is important to keep an open mind, enjoy what we find good (even though we may paint in a different manner) and to PAINT.

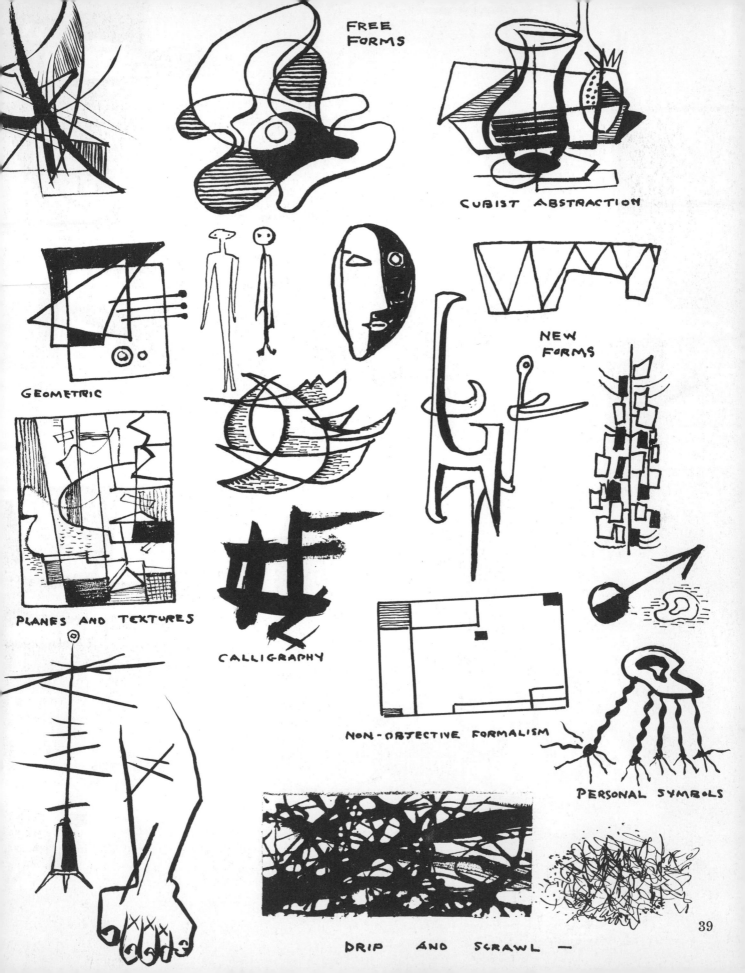

FREE
FORMS

CUBIST ABSTRACTION

GEOMETRIC

NEW
FORMS

PLANES AND TEXTURES

CALLIGRAPHY

NON-OBJECTIVE FORMALISM

PERSONAL SYMBOLS

39

DRIP AND SCRAWL —

LINEAR MOVEMENT IN COMPOSITION

Learning to select and use lines and shapes from nature is not as difficult as it may seem. The important thing to remember is this: take, leave or add to fill your picture space with areas which are not monotonous, but will function as a complete unit to satisfy the eye. You should not be able to take away the smallest area or line from a well-knit unit without missing it.

Even in your first struggles with composition you will begin to see and feel what func-

tions well and what doesn't. Much of your planning will be made from intuition—this area doesn't seem to sit right, or this line seems "out-of-joint." Sensitiveness to space-filling will come with practice; studying successful compositions of others will help you. There are a number of time-honored rules which may, at first, be of value, but more often than not they will not seem to apply to the particular problem you have in hand. You will be told that it is bad to cut a canvas

UNITY

RELATED LINE MOVEMENT

DISPERSAL

UNRELATED MOVEMENT

See page 145 for
Casein technique

across the exact middle. As a general rule this is so, as it automatically divides your picture into two equal, and therefore monotonous areas. Then later you may see a picture which has gone out of its way to break this rationalization—and it works!

One of the chief reasons for failure in sketching out a composition in line and mass which holds together all over, is that the beginner does not understand the power of line movement at his command. Lines and areas can be manipulated and directed to take the onlooker's eye across, through, and around a sequence of points of interest. As soon as we make individual lines or lines bounding areas on the flat surface of our picture surface, we set up tensions and thrusts for the eye to follow. These can be drawn to lead the eye from the edges of the picture (the unimportant area) to more important areas. They can pick up a point here, encircle it, and move on to a main focal point on which the whole composition pivots. Or the lines can be put down in such a way as to distress us, or lead us from corners of the picture directly out of the picture plane before we have managed to get into it.

This movement on the surface is further complicated when we begin to deal with composition in depth. Here we are concerned with what happens to the movements of our eye as it sorts out the volumes and solids we have suggested on our flat two-dimensional surface. We will discuss this further in the next section. For the time being, we will think only of the *pattern movement* set up as shown in sketch above. The arrows indicate the circular movements within the picture area. The anchor or pivot for these directional movements is encircled. This is not evident in the photograph. The added pole, the shortening of the fishing-shed, and other changes were made in *making a composition from the facts.* The four illustrations shown below the photograph were other test sketches to analyze the material awaiting our use.

Exercises such as these will help you in sorting out more complicated and difficult subjects. A few hours of experimenting from photographic material which you have taken yourself can provide you with plenty of fun. Use tracing paper over the photographs and try and discover what the main linear movements are. Freely drawn brush drawings, (opposite) in which you use sections only, will help train your sense of selection.

MOVEMENT IN DEPTH

We are dealing here with a most complicated subject, one about which there are many contradictory facets. We can only hint and suggest here some of the basic tenets of the theory of space organization in picture making. If you are interested in studying the problem further, several useful books are listed in the Appendix.

Not only do we have movements of line and mass, as we showed in the previous pages, on the *surface* of our picture, but we have also the problem of controlling the balance and movements of the eye back through the picture-space, behind the picture plane. As soon as we take *three* dimensional objects and impose upon them the limitations of *two* dimensions, we enter a new world of spatial

organization. Surface pattern, plus the satisfying unity of these tensions and movements set up in depth, brings about new problems of composing—problems which have intrigued artists ever since Cezanne devoted his life to the search for integrated form.

The illustrations may help make the theory clearer. The picture plane is shown as the flat front of a box or a stage. This is the area where we set up movements, tensions, thrusts, as soon as we indicate solids or volumes. Parts of these solids function as part of the picture plane (i.e. the flat negative areas which are parallel to the picture plane.) Other areas are turned at an angle to the P.P. These are *dynamic* planes, moving our eye back into picture space. The interplay between these active and static areas sets up movement and tensions.

To bind these into a satisfactory visual whole, and at the same time incorporate the flat-surface pattern of our objects on the picture plane, is the keynote of spatial organization. This is the meaning of the phrase "respect the integrity of the two-dimensional picture plane" which crops up so frequently in art school lectures and teaching.

The understanding and application of these theories can be most useful in giving structure to your pictures. A too intellectualized pursuit of the space-concept theory and a preoccupation with its demands can quickly turn your work into mental exercises, too often obvious, and derivative. It was with considerable reason that an over-zealous group of followers of the theory were called in derision, a few years ago—"space cadets".

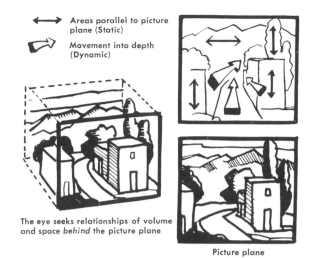

The eye seeks relationships of volume and space *behind* the picture plane

The illustration above shows with small arrows the *static* planes. The larger arrows show the movement back into space, behind the picture plane.

LOW TIDE

A painting made to experiment with shifting planes and volume emphasis. Here the picture-plane surface has been "respected," its flatness preserved.

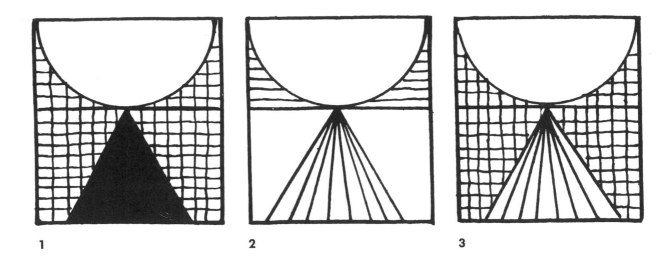

1   2   3

THE CONFUSION OF TERMS

The terms "picture plane," "space," "spatial relationships," etc. are often confusing to the student. The diagrams shown here attempt to clarify them.

No. 1. Think of this as a flat triangle balancing a flat half-circle. Both forms are on the *flat surface of the picture plane*.

No. 2. Now we have persective lines running down a road to a horizon and rising moon. The road is assumed to be going back into *pictorial space*.

No. 3. A combination of both diagrams. The eye tries to establish relationships, but is confused. The grill tells us that the surface is flat, the road pierces the picture plane. An unpleasant uncertainty, visually, is set up.

No. 4. In this we set out a simple form. Is it a box in perspective, or a house with a dormer roof?

No. 5. A simple optical illusion is set up by the contradictions of an object which appears to be parallel to the picture plane—for one moment—and then becomes an object *in depth*. Is this a house with a flat roof and a chimney at the far end or an object parallel to the *picture plane*?

No. 6. Here we emphasize the *flatness of the picture plane* with arbitrary horizontal and vertical lines. On this surface we project our simple form. Our picture plane now contains *flat pattern on the surface* and also takes our eye *back* into the picture plane. *Tensions and balance* in *space are created*, but the *two-dimensional nature* of the paper's surface has been stressed.

Negative space, equivalent space, tensions, thrusts, static and dead planes; the list is unending. All of the terms have sprung into being to rationalize the phenomena of creating or rejecting the illusions of three-dimensional objects on a flat surface, on our paper or canvas.

You may paint away happily and creatively all your life without even knowing these terms or their implications. The chances are, however, that research into the problem will strengthen and help your work to be structurally sound and visually satisfying.

4   5   6

AND PICTORIAL SPACE

FORMS AND PLANES STRESSED

47

DYNAMIC AND CALM

ROCKS, SEA AND SUNSET

The use of dynamic lines and strong forms to emphasize movement and shifting light are apparent. A rapid sketch of this kind, in which the over-all effect is achieved by sacrificing needless detail to impact of mood, makes exciting painting, especially when you are dodging flying spray! Some casein white was used over the watercolor.

HORIZONTALS
(REPOSE)

DIAGONALS
(ACTION)

VERTICALS
(DIGNITY)

CURVES
(GAY)

EVENING HARBOR

The effect was reversed in this sketch. Horizontal lines of the calm, late-evening mood were stressed to give a quiet, peaceful impression. Here the technique and handling of the watercolor was made consistent with the effect desired. Let the subject bring out its own technique and form.

SELECTION AND EMPHASIS OF YOUR SUBJECT

Here is a more complicated subject than the street photograph we used to dissect for our "sense of form" illustration, on Page 30. See if you can isolate forms in the same manner—houses, wharf, lobster pots, etc.

The photograph is already a composition, as we selected a pleasing viewpoint for the camera, and chose the best placing of lights and darks within the limitations of the lens sight. But this is only a beginning for the artist. We have the advantage of selecting and emphasizing any area, we can strengthen or weaken dominant masses, and plan our tonal scheme as we wish.

We may decide that the lobster pots fight for interest with the dark sheds in the background. One must predominate. We can add boats or items of interest which are nearby, we can enliven the water plane by stressing its flatness. There is no limit to the possibilities we can take from the subject.

Two approaches are shown here. The first is almost a literal transcription though the lobster pots have been subdued and made less important. More sky has beeen added, and the direction of the poles and ropes changed.

The second sketch is a much more lively analysis. It is a stronger pictorial statement.

If we can keep this structural plan, adding enrichment of color, detail and texture, it will be the more successful of the two.

Try your own composition using the lobster pots as the main theme this time. It will demand a new conception and order of elements. Make the sheds a secondary interest. Try this in one color, Payne's gray or black, eight by ten inches. Concentrate on the spotting of darks. Even the placing and spotting of the gulls must be thought out carefully. Nothing in a good picture organization is thrown in haphazardly. Notice the useful repetition of the slats of the lobster pots repeating the vertical logs along the sides of the wharf.

The white spaces of paper have been used to advantage in this sketch. Foreground objects are spotted in with stronger design than in the sketch above. The pulley and iron arm have been placed at the top left-hand corner to help bring the eye back into the picture. Notice the diagonal line across the water which helps define this area spatially. This is much more "alive" than our first rendering.

"Nantucket Boats" shown on Page 49 is a watercolor painted out of doors. Its composition was plotted out in a similar manner to the exercise you have just finished. The original sketch for it is shown on Page 102.

VERACRUZ MORNING

A direct watercolor painted on the spot in the fishing village of Alvarado near Veracruz. Painted rapidly on a thin, warm-tinted Michelet charcoal drawing paper, there was no opportunity for retouching, scraping or patching up mistakes. This kind of watercolor depends entirely on its spontaneous qualities for unity. Everything has to work the first time. If, under the excitement of the moment, the painting gets out of hand, the washes out of control, there is only one thing to do; start over on another piece of paper.

When a rapid impression of this kind does come off it is a rewarding sensation which makes up for lots of failures. If you have been out working early in the morning, you'll go back to a hearty breakfast with a fine appetite and a glow of satisfaction. The Japanese masters were well aware of the charm of spontaneity in their work. And they knew how necessary the previous study and practice were before the magic moment of actual execution. Years of training and observation allowed the most talented to paint their magnificent brush drawings in an incredibly short time. I have watched a renowned Japanese painter fill a six-foot long scroll with galloping horses and mountain pines—action, movement and exquisite composition. It was completed in less than fifteen minutes with every stroke and dot of the brush unfalteringly placed. How right and how simple it seemed. And how much more than just *technique* came out of the end of the brush! Later, when I spoke with him I learned that he had been studying and drawing horses daily for forty years, trying to solve the secret of their beautiful lines.

Some years ago, James Bowie wrote a book which is worth studying, if you can find a copy of it. *On the Laws of Japanese Painting* was written after many years of study with famous artists in Japan. In it he gives the seventy-two laws for painting, describing the rigid discipline of training. And he states that nothing is more constantly urged upon the artist's attention than the great underlying principle that it is impossible to express in art what one does not first feel. The precept was frequently repeated in the lines:

> Our spirit must make our hand its servitor;
> Our hand must respond to each behest of our spirit.

ORCHESTRATION

The semantics of the painting world are often ambiguous and confusing. The division between what is "decorative," for example, and finely "creative" is often no more than a personal like or dislike. "Romanticism" is a fluctuating quality and the tagging of what is an "expressionist" or a "formalist" changes with the yearly crop of art critics' reviews.

As I gathered together the sections we have been discussing under the term of "composition", an analogy came to mind which may be of value to you the next time you bring together your lines, masses, colors and forms to make a picture. It may clarify the task for you if you will accept the larger connotation of the word.

Think of a fine orchestra. Each man is capable of being a soloist, of giving a one-man performance of the highest quality. Imagine if, when they are assembled, each insists on holding the spotlight. There would be no *pianissimos,* no melodic line would emerge from the chaos of instruments all calling attention to themselves by listening only to themselves. The over-all harmony would be sacrificed to the individual part.

So often this happens to our pictures. See

to it that we—the conductor—call our players in at the right time and as part of the whole performance. If the corner of our picture—a fine, singing note of red—attracts too much attention, it will conflict with the equally vivid note of the same size and timbre elsewhere. One or the other must give way.

The instruments of our picture-making, the straight and curved lines, the oppositions of light and dark, our color harmonies, all these can serve us well or cause us to end up with visual chaos. No matter how skillful and tempting the particular section is, out it must go, or be modified, if it does not contribute to the larger conception. And at times it takes courage and ruthlessness to subdue a particularly fine spot of color or drawing.

Opposite are shown the workings of an orchestrated sketch. No. 1 is a sketch made to collect facts drawn on the spot. No. 2 is a black-and-white layout tying together the parts into a stronger design, each part relating to the other. No. 3 is a watercolor painted from sketch No. 2. The basic patterns are kept while adding color, varied number of tones and added textures.

3

1

2

STILL LIFE

JUGS AND BOTTLES

Learning to seek *beyond* the ordinary sight of objects to the exciting elements waiting for our picture-making, requires much practice and self-training.

One positive way of helping our "artist's eye" is to paint a number of studies from still-life objects, using the simplest of forms. Most of these can be found in profusion around us—a plate or jug, a cup, a pineapple, or a few books and a candlestick. With these we are able to settle down to work, without the annoyances of onlookers, changes of weather, flies or dust, which plague us so often out of doors. We can take our time arrange our objects in some kind of satisfy ing order before we start, keeping the group intact until we are finished with it.

The principle thing we must keep in mind in an exercise of this kind is, *why* are we painting these objects. The whole value of this session will be lost if we look upon it as a chore of sitting down only to copy the objects accurately and photographically. Certainly this can have its value as well, and there will be times when we will do just that to train our eye and hand to mechanically assess proportion and tone and color relationships. The story is told by one of Matisse's students of his bewilderment during his first lesson, when the Master set him down to draw from a plaster cast with instructions to make an accurate and faithful copy. He had hoped to be handed a pail of "Matisse pink" and a "Fauve" brush, not the discipline of academic training. It was only later, when he saw the delineations of careful copies by Matisse from the old masters, that he realized he had a long way to go.

But today we are not thinking of copying. This is an exercise in different terms and we'll leave you to do the plaster-cast drawing later.

Here then, is your problem. You are not setting out to make a literal transcription, even if you *are* capable of doing so, nor are you going to make a colored photograph. You are using shapes, lines and color on a flat surface, and the group you set up will be the excuse, the starting point for any combination which you may construct. This does not mean jumbling up forms, turning vases upside down because they will look different from what is in front of you. The objects you see are to start you thinking, the suggestion on which you are able to make your design grow. You will have to modify the group, change it where it is dull, elongate or invent forms where necessary. No matter how tastefully you have arranged your group on the table, your real problem only begins when you take the brush in hand and start to paint. Then the sketch must grow into a life of its own, after the reality before you. Your jugs, violins, apples must now begin to live their new lives as part of your picture.

That juicy apple is now a painter's apple, a far different object than a real apple. Now it becomes paint and texture, a space on your surface which must relate as an element to all the other elements on your paper.

The degree of abstraction you choose to use depends upon you. The further you take the group from reality, the more you must know how to extract the essential essence.

The sketchbook will help you, as always. Quick charcoal drawings on large sheets of paper will also be useful.

To point out the enjoyment to be had from this kind of exercise is not easy to do with words. If I could show you personally, by a demonstration of still-life painting, what exciting worlds are to be found in two or three objects, my task would be simpler. All I can ask of you is that you put yourself in the frame of mind where you will look through and beyond the objects to the opportunity of creating (with talent and luck) something which could be creative painting. If you are in doubt about this, look over the work of all the giants of painting over the last century, or consider how many fine works of art of today spring from the contemplation of inanimate objects.

Braque, Juan Gris and Picasso predicated

"Easter Table" (p. 37) was painted from this spot sketch

their whole movement in the early days on such homely objects as the pipe, a few books or a bowl of fruit. What they did with such ordinary objects (and still do) keeps the art-book lover poor and the printmaker constantly busy.

A few more admonitions and you are ready to start.

Remember, you can, if you wish, employ two or more points of view in your picture. There is nothing to stop you looking *down* and from the *side* as well, if you wish. You may draw your objects as though you can see through them, if it strengthens your design. Distort your shapes if by doing so you gain more force and character in your picture. Be extremely careful of your background shapes. Make these an integral part of your whole picture. They must function and not be "dead" areas on which objects appear to be stuck. Go all out with your textures and color once you have decided on the construction of your sketch. Use your color-mixing knowledge to obtain an over-all unity. If you are painting in watercolor, call on all your techniques to enrich the painting, but remember that technical virtuosity is always secondary to the expression of your personal feelings and ideas.

1. *A careful outline of objects made to study shapes and relative proportions. Group bottles, jugs and other objects into a simple arrangement. You are not concerned with "self-expression" here, only a purely mechanical discipline to train your eye and hand. Use brush or pen outline.*

2. *A few washes of black water-color to study tone values. How dark is the yellow jug when compared with the dark green bottle and rendered in the black and white tonal scale? Keep the grays few in number and avoid over-modelling. Use the white paper as the lightest value. Paint over your outlined drawing.*

3. *No hard outline this time. Try this on textured water-color paper. Emphasize forms by putting dark accents behind light ones, light areas behind dark. Vary your edges by painting with water only and dropping in darks to give you soft gradations. Lift off darks by moistening with water and picking color up with clean dry brush. This is fine practice for control of washes and judging how light paint will appear when dry. You might try this exercise in full color in the same manner.*

4. *A freely drawn rough based on the still-life group. Here we modify the shapes, areas are broken up, lines and masses suggested by the objects in space are carried through and tied up with the flat surface of the picture plane. Let your imagination work. Break away from the visual appearance, making the*

objects the means of inventive picture-making. You'll find this much harder to do than it looks!

5. Textures and movement of planes are stressed in a further development from No. 4. Lights and darks must lead from one to another in an exciting visual pattern. Now we have the beginning of what might become a creative painting. Semi-abstract, not too far removed from the facts, yet more vital than the dull reporting of the first three interpretations. Try your sketch at this stage in a carefully planned color scheme.

FLOWERS

There is hardly a painter of contemporary note who has not studied and worked at the problem of using flower forms for creative work—Chagall, Vlaminck, Bonnard, Demuth, Hartley, Watkins, to name a few.

Whether it be the single study of a blossom or a composition derived from an elaborate flower arrangement, the subject has always intrigued artists. It is not by accident that some of our most powerful painters have added to their reputations by using motifs taken from a cluster of blossoms in a vase, or from plant forms.

What was said in the previous still-life lesson applies to the flower subject. Study the work of painters to see what has been accomplished in this field. Avoid the photographic drawing and obvious coloring seen so often. Entice from your material lines and forms which will give your study some feeling of growing, living plants.

Try sketching in ink on a slightly moist paper, letting the pen line soften and run on the wet ground. Add washes of diluted color before the paper dries. Or, try the complete color painting when your eye catches an arrangement which delights you.

The color print opposite is reproduced from a picture painted partly from memory the morning after I had glimpsed the flowers in the half-light of evening. The theme, "Night Flowers" was an effort to catch the feeling of living, colored forms in a subdued and evocative light. It was painted in casein, with glazes to enrich it. In it I tried to take the flowers beyond the facts of vision, yet have them retain their flower forms and colors.

LEONARD
BROOK.

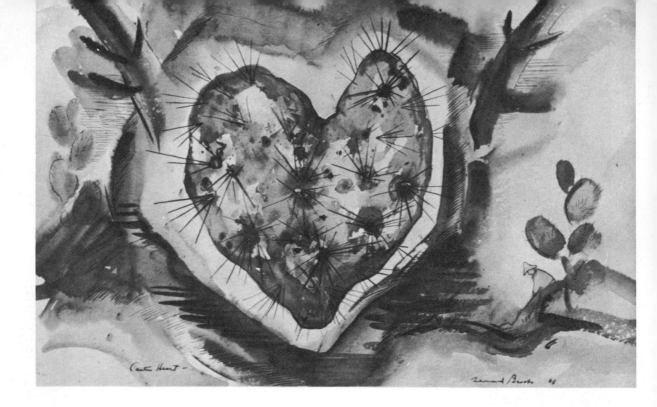

"The Cactus Heart" was drawn with pen and ink, with washes superimposed. The pleasure of drawing and painting from such material is unlimited, and if we lack a garden or leafy branch, a pot of ivy will serve us. The search for form, the study of the convolutions of a leaf or blossom, will provide us with an entrancing world in itself.

The page of pencil flower outlines was made in an afternoon's stroll in the garden. Careful, almost botanical drawings of this nature will help you to understand the underlying structure and design possibilities of flowers. Such research need not be a chore and will reward you with a truer understanding of your subject-matter when you concentrate on less literal interpretation.

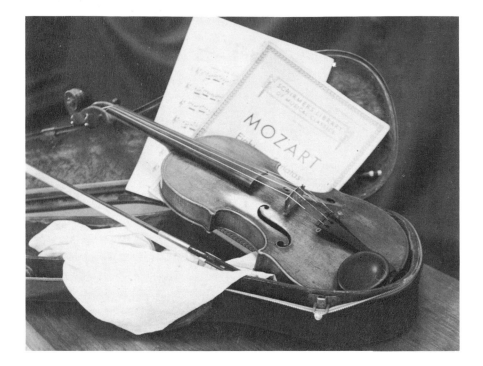

TAKE WHAT YOU NEED

In his *Treatise on Landscape Painting*, Andre Lhote makes the profound statement: "Everything you want is to be found in nature but you have to be educated enough to want to find only what is required."

Educated, of course, as an artist, and naturally, the "what is required" will vary with the temperament of the individual and what he is seeking. A tree will serve as a starting point for one man while another will use figures or combinations of figures for a lifetime of work—as did the late Reginald Marsh with his Bowery and Follies paintings. Cezanne found "what is required" to make many of his great pictures from a few apples.

As an exercise in taking what is required from what is there, I have selected a violin in its case. As a photograph it has the beginnings of an arrangement, but when we consider it as material for a composition and as the source of a picture, it will take on many modifications. As we work on it, one area will

demand tying up with another, movements of the eye back into the picture plane will not function as we want them to, in places (such as the strong white of the line of the bow) the directional thrusts will carry our eye too strongly out of the picture with no return movement. Large areas of white (the cloth in the violin case for example) absorb too much attention without giving back interesting passages; there will be dead areas of "negative space," background areas flatly unrelated to the curving movements of violin and case.

Thinking in color, our problem would be different. The sheet music, yellow and green, would not dominate as thoroughly as it does when shown only in black and white, and the crimson lining of the case would influence the handling of the right-hand corner. But as we are thinking of this exercise in black and white values only, this will determine our break-up of space.

The violin has been elongated and the repe-

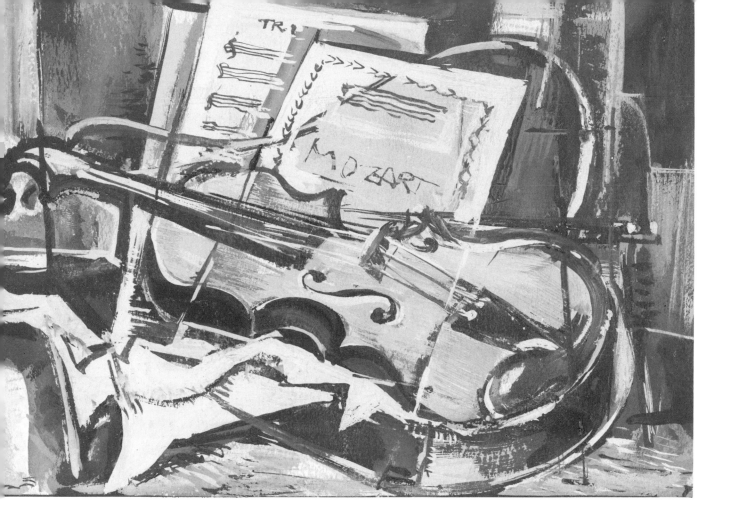

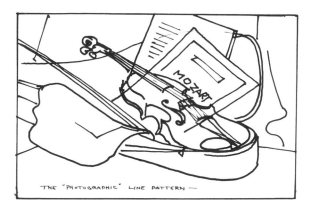

THE "PHOTOGRAPHIC" LINE PATTERN —

EXPERIMENTAL BREAK-UP OF SPACE + PATTERN

tition of curves emphasized. The white cloth has been strengthened with angles placed in opposition and next to the violin's curved sides and beautiful "S" holes. Planes have been flattened out, overlapping lines have controlled the recession by bringing forward areas to the picture-plane surface. The music, for example, has lines running through and cutting across the violin planes. The same indictation of the case through the music helps to stop a falling-back or concave feeling, which is the weakness of the photograph.

Wherever monotonous areas have disturbed the over-all unity of the design, lines, planes and areas have been brought into being to relate these areas to the rest of the scheme.

STUDIO INTERIOR

This was painted on David Cox paper with dampened surface and colors washed in. A few definitive lines were put in after the paper was dry.

A tracing over the picture will give you the underlying design which is based on the white frame leaning against the table. This rectangular form is the starting point on which the other lines and planes move.

Easel, chair, plant and window have been spotted out to give the maximum interest. A photograph of this corner of the room would be visually accurate and dull. Though the sketch is not an exact copy of the studio, it does convey, in color, the feeling of morning light, and more importantly for me, my particular reaction to the place, in terms of design and color.

SOME TECHNICAL MEANS

1. *Painted on smooth, cheap drawing paper. This can be used with clean direct washes but will not stand overpainting. Double-line scratches put in with the broken edge of a razor blade. Dark rocks are almost opaque with heavy pigment.*

2. *Rubber cement or Maskoid can be useful. The water is blocked out first with free broken brush strokes using the cement brush. Green and blue water is painted over this. When dry the cement is removed with a soft eraser leaving the white paper showing through. Tricky, and too often an obvious device.* ⟶

3. *Sunlit wood interiors are confusing subjects but always challenging material for the sketcher. This sketch is an example of using sandpaper and a sharp knife to pick out lights and enrich the textures.*

4. *A water fountain sparkling against rich green foliage. This was done on smooth illustration board which did not break the brush-strokes or leave white "spottings" which are useful in some subjects. The white of the water was then picked out with a razor blade. Use this technique in the painting of subjects like the "Waterfall" on page 101.* ⟶

GRADATED INTENSITY SCALE

Seeing color is a highly individual thing, and although the final result is *your* choice and taste, you must have a clear understanding of the possibilities of your palette. It can take many months of undirected mixing and daubing before you find out what colors sit well together, which ones have a tendency to go muddy or sour, what colors modify others into subtle in-between colors, which are more transparent and opaque, etc.

Although it may look like a chore, I highly recommend a study and duplication of the chart reproduced here. It is not easy to make, will take care and time, but it will show you more about watercolor in a few hours than weeks of experimental picture making.

Its purpose is this: to give you the feel of individual pigments, their various intensities, from the watered-down delicate tints to the strongest saturation you can load into your brush without picking up pigment straight from the tube. It will show you how some colors combine with others, changing them with a mere hint of pigment; it will show you how light or dark a pigment can become.

With more space the chart would have included all the colors which you might use at anytime: Hooker's green, cobalt violet, thalo blue, etc. I have kept it to the essential primaries; reds, blues and yellows, but there is no reason why you should not draw up other charts of a similar kind using opposites, or showing various ways of making greens with every color *but* green. Using green is one of the pitfalls of the amateur, one which can set the paper swimming with sickly or poisonous color faster than any other. Try making greens from ochres and blues, yellow and cobalt, yellow and cerulean, umbers and blues, for the richest and most subtle greens can be made from these mixtures.

To make this chart, rule up one inch squares on a heavy quality, stretched paper or pad. Paint graduated strips of color horizontally across the page using a brush well-loaded with pigment first, gradually adding more water and brushing this right across the page as evenly as you can. Do this with each color listed, letting the strip dry before you do the next to avoid one running into the other, or leaving a strip while the upper one is drying. Then turn the board and paint the vertical strips across the page horizontally. Keep the board at a slight angle to aid the color in running downward.

As you do this you will notice the paint you are using picking up the color of the first strip you painted, and mixing. Pay no attention to this, but try and paint directly without going back or scrubbing into the paper.

When you have completed all the strips, you can see where the diagonal line crossing from corner to corner of the chart has given you the most intense and pure blocks of the colors, cadmium red over cadmium red, blues over blues, etc. On each side of the diagonal center line are squares with modifications of the pure color mixed with yellows, blues, etc. When completed, square up the strips with a broad pen-nib and india ink and you will have a chart suggesting numberless shades and tints from two color mixtures. You will have experienced too, how some colors have more covering power than others, how some *stain* the paper and some seem to lay on the surface of the paper. You will note how colors, when wet, look almost like different colors compared to when they are dry, and also how much lighter they become.

At the side of the chart I have shown several neutrals made by mixing opposites, or complementaries. Try other mixtures of this kind. They will provide you with rich lively grays and darks *without* using blacks. Be sure and saturate the water with plenty of pigment to obtain maximum richness.

Though it will take some patience, it is worth doing this chart carefully. Pin it up over your work table. It will be of help to you and remind you that watercolor need not be the washed out delicate medium many consider it to be.

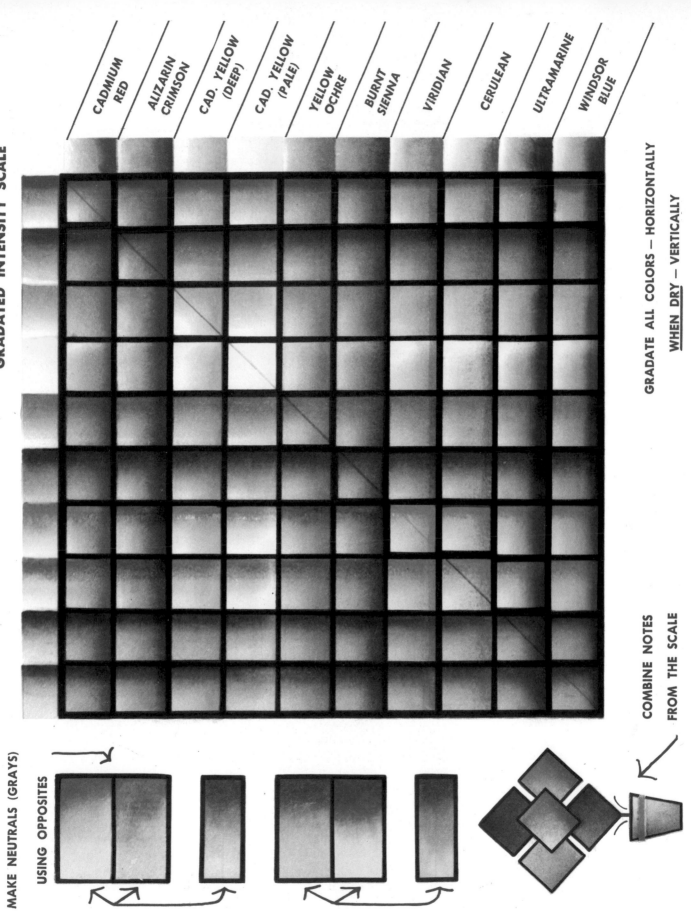

GRADATED INTENSITY SCALE

CADMIUM RED
ALIZARIN CRIMSON
CAD. YELLOW (DEEP)
CAD. YELLOW (PALE)
YELLOW OCHRE
BURNT SIENNA
VIRIDIAN
CERULEAN
ULTRAMARINE
WINDSOR BLUE

GRADATE ALL COLORS — HORIZONTALLY

WHEN <u>DRY</u> — VERTICALLY

COMBINE NOTES

FROM THE SCALE

MAKE NEUTRALS (GRAYS)

USING OPPOSITES

TEXTURES

Elsewhere in this book I have written and demonstrated some of the textural possibilities of watercolor. Illustrated above is the kind of landscape subject which will enable you to practice this important part of your means. Since painting a fine watercolor, because it requires a combination of drawing, painting, composing, handling washes, textures, and expressive brushwork simultaneously, is often like juggling six balls and three plates, we are wise to settle on one phase of the art at a time. Take a morning to concentrate on one element.

The exercise above was done without too much thought of composition. Make up your own landscape if you wish, including in it a variety of nature's infinite textures. Sky, rocks, mountains, seaweed and shifting light. Each of these will give you a chance for texture-making. Make the rocks *feel* like rocks, not like a pile of hay or earth; try to give the water the feeling of water—choppy or smooth—the seaweed dank and sodden.

On the spot observation will help you to develop an intimate knowledge of such qualities, but much of your study can be done with watercolor in your own studio. Try variations of brush strokes, wet and dry passages, soft and hard edges. Study the techniques of original paintings by others. Notice the smooth and rough brush work, the direction of strokes to express form and modeling. And don't worry about style. You will develop your own in much the same way as your handwriting has its own distinctive character.

WINTER HARBOR

Do not make an obsession of using the razor blade for every sketch. Occasionally it is invaluable, a legitimate addition to your means. Here it was used to scratch out rough strokes of light suggestive of snow and ice in various sections of the picture. It was not used as a "patch-up" device. Its use was planned before beginning the picture.

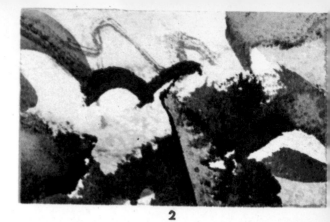

1

2

3

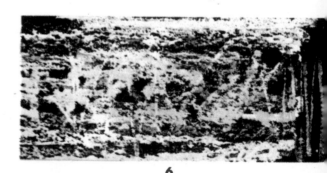

4

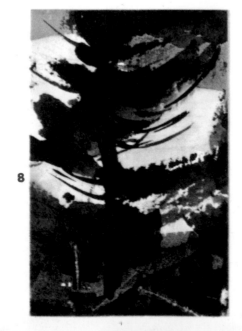

5

6

7

8

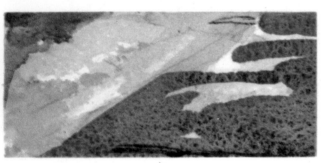

9

FURTHER METHODS

The small sections reproduced on Page 74 are taken from large watercolors and shown actual size to give some more ideas of the handling of transparent watercolor. When you have completed the Intensity Chart, try similar experimental sections.

It is essential to know the properties of various papers and their textures. On Page 95 there is a chart of a number of standard surfaces showing the variety of rough and smooth papers you can choose from, and what happens to your color on them. The reproductions here should prove to you that watercolor need not be a thin, washed-out media. It is possible to get much more depth and strength of color than you think, without painting over or getting muddy color.

1. Note depth of saturation of darks. The very intense violet was made with ultramarine and alizarin crimson. Thalo blue or prussian blue is even darker but has a tendency to be hard and too dominant unless very much modified by such colors as burnt sienna or umbers.

2. Black was frowned upon for many years by watercolor purists. It does have a way of dirtying colors unless skillfully used and not overmixed. At first it is better to learn how to neutralize your colors with the complementaries or opposites as demonstrated on Page 71. Today, black is very much in favor and you will see it used to good purpose in many watercolors. I carry it in my paintbox but seldom use it. Payne's gray, a cold bluish black serves to make the grays I prefer. No. 2 is black watercolor with razor blade pressed flat to scrape down to paper texture.

3. A smooth drawing paper. India ink (indelible) is used first to draw in outlines, then washes laid on top—a very useful way of making colored notes. The drawing holds the watercolor together and the washes on top provide reference to the color for later development. Washes must be direct, once over, and not scrubbed at, as the paper is easily damaged.

4. A spatter with watercolor over a semidry wash. Tap the brush lightly after it is loaded with paint. Experiment with this first and make sure that there is not too much water in the brush. Flick, tap and drop spots of color into the wash already there. The illustration on Page 94 shows how use was made of this technique to break up foreground. Be sure and mask the rest of sketch with scrap paper first, and make sure there are no clean mounts or other watercolors nearby! This is a variation of many ways of dropping in sand, or even salt while washes are wet and brushing it off after the wash is dry to obtain sandy, grainy textures.

5. A float of cobalt blue over a warm, dry undertone of ochre with a hint of alizarin crimson. This will give you a transparent vibrant shadow color as the heavier pigment of cobalt sinks into the valleys of a rough textured paper. This was a favorite device of the academic English watercolor school. A granulated wash, it can give a flat wash character by producing two colors vibrating in one wash over the white paper. Try other colors such as cerulean or cobalt violet with warm washes of sienna (raw and burnt), and the umbers. Also try warm washes over cool.

6. Yellow and white crayon over rough paper first and color on top. Scratch through to wax while washes are wet or when dry. This technique of wax repellent and color can be seen at the top of Page 94. Be sure and test the perman-

ence of other wax crayons if you wish to use them. Most crayons, even the most brilliant reds and mauves, will fade away completely in a few weeks of sunlight. Prepare a card of crayon strokes; cover over half, leaving the other half exposed to the sun. You will be amazed at the disappearance of some of your strokes in a short time. *Use only unfading colors.*

7. A section from a market place sketch where there were many small figures to suggest. Here is a case where the yellow and vermillion is put on thickly, almost opaque. In small areas this can be done without spoiling the consistent transparent quality of the rest of the picture. A fine brush was used over loose washes to suggest details.

8. Try to paint your darks in one painting, especially in tree forms and foliage such as this pine. Then drop in more color while wet if you see the color is drying too lightly. Load the brush well with pigment. And remember to judge well ahead of time how your darks dry several tones lighter than when the washes are wet. Notice the one-stroke broken edge of pine bough against the sky.

9. There are some "stain" colors which seem to penetrate the paper more than others. Remember the color chart exercise and how certain colors such as alizarin crimson, viridian and windsor blue dyed the paper more than the opaque cadmiums and ochres. Take advantage of this by covering the paper with a darker color than you need, then squeeze the color aside with a razor blade and lift off left-over color with a brush. This whole section was painted dark and the lights lifted off in this manner exposing the crimson stain underneath.

10. White and yellow wax crayons were used on warm tinted paper with washes of blue and green over the crayon and a spatter pattern over foreground in dark watercolor. Finally, pen and India ink outlined the boat shapes. (See Page 94) This was done several years later from a fairly accurate drawing made at night in California. The subject is an excuse to invent exciting visual agitations of line, speckles and textures, and a use of accidental effects. The "accidents" however were controlled and preconceived to a considerable extent beforehand.

WINTER FOREGROUND

The subtleties of a simple foreground are not easy to paint, nor the effect of thousands of twigs against the sky. Nothing reveals the amateur so quickly as passages of this kind. Careful drawings of brush and branch forms will help you master these areas where a quick flick of the brush must suggest enough for the eye and imagination to fill in the rest. Think first—then put it down simply and directly.

LOOSE OR TIGHT HANDLING?

I have indicated before that there is no one way of handling watercolor. If you wish to use it in a tight, built-up manner, placing stroke over stroke with a small brush, there is no reason why you should not do so. And if you want to pour it on with a watering can and shaving brush, you are free to do so. It is the end result which is important, not how you accomplished it.

The sketch below was done in the first manner. Washes were put on, scrubbed out, repainted with small strokes. The roof of the

hut and the decorative rendering of the palm leaves were built up in this way.

Notice the broken planes cutting through the mountain and on the right-hand edge of the picture. This was done to give a feeling of the tropic light moving in from the dawn and to connect the sky and water forms with the rest of the picture by bringing forward the background planes.

Integrating the sky with the rest of the landscape is one of the problems you will constantly face. Each picture will demand its

own solution. Sometimes you may find cloud forms and lines which will tie into the rest of your composition. Generally you will be forced to invent these lines, discovering where they must be, as your picture grows. (See page 143)

A study of the watercolors of John Marin will show you a master's solution to making a "wholeness" of separate elements of a land-scape. To make your picture function, each part complementing the other, is a task which can be solved only by constant experiment and study and the development of your sensitivity to space-filling.

"Janitzio," above, is an example of the loose and spontaneous technique. The orchestration of parts was more important in this sketch than the manner of handling.

LEARN WHAT THE
BRUSH CAN DO

Learn to know what your brushes are capable of doing for you. Practice varieties of strokes and markings on discarded papers until you can control the textures at will. This is not to cultivate tricks or mannerisms. Using a brush to "write" your symbols must become as easy as writing your own name with a pen. The sooner you learn this art, the sooner your watercolors will have that fluid sure touch which is one of the charms of watercolor.

An actual-size detail of brush handling of tree trunk and leaf clusters. Notice varieties of wet, semi-dry and combined techniques shown on opposite page. Also the slow-fast strokes.

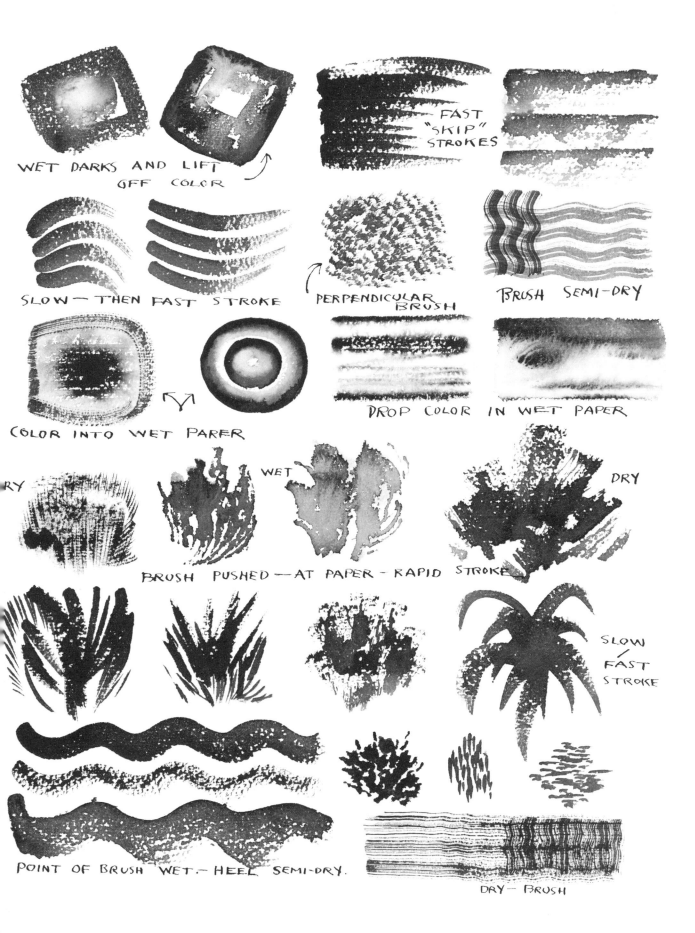

WET DARKS AND LIFT
OFF COLOR

FAST "SKIP" STROKES

SLOW — THEN FAST STROKE

PERPENDICULAR BRUSH

BRUSH SEMI-DRY

COLOR INTO WET PAPER

DROP COLOR IN WET PAPER

RY

WET

DRY

BRUSH PUSHED — AT PAPER — RAPID STROKE

SLOW / FAST STROKE

POINT OF BRUSH WET — HEEL SEMI-DRY.

DRY — BRUSH

ONE COLOR WASH

Blazing light and dark shadows give us an opportunity to indicate solidity of form. All in-between values are more or less eliminated, in the felt-pen sketch above.

It is an excellent exercise for using a one-color wash drawing. Using sepia, black, or Payne's gray, we can translate our quick notation into a watercolor.

Freely brushed, painted directly with no pencil indications, the broad strokes were painted in such a way that white spots were left here and there in the washes, giving a sparkle to large simple areas. The ground planes were left as white paper to give the lightest tone suggestive of bleached high-keyed sunlight.

The shadow areas themselves were not painted too dark to give a quality of reflected light thrown back from the ground. Notice too, how the small spots and dashes on the large areas of white walls relieve the monotony of much white space and at the same time indicate the adobe nature of wall and brick. It is necessary to pick out these accents very carefully. Too much repetition can cause unimportant areas to be agitated and attract too much attention.

Try painting similar arrangements of high-keyed buildings with strong, simple lighting. Use a large, flat brush and one small pointed sable for drawing in after the large

washes are dry. Make the white paper work for you by *planning your white areas first* as in the felt-pen sketch.

A general effect of freshness and directness should be your aim in this exercise. Give yourself half-an-hour at the most to finish it.

SHRIMP FISHERMAN

A Chinese-like subject painted on the Pacific Mexican coast from pencil notes made by full moon. Painted with sepia watercolor, it provided an excellent exercise in varied brush work. White paper was used for water reflections and the darks in the large trees were made with the fullest possible saturation of color without painting muddy or opaque darks. Chinese brushes, ranging from a large wash brush to a small pointed writing brush were used throughout. The sketch depends on its tonal contrasts for mood. Large areas of lightest tone value were painted first, gradually working toward the darkest area and final detailed accents of figures, hut textures.

I once had some fine results with a sketch class by having them study their subject for ten minutes and then turn their backs on it to paint it. Having to fix basic forms in their minds without being confused with a thousand and one superfluous facts forced the students to retain essentials only. Try it!

New Brunswick Bay

LET'S PAINT

We've covered a lot of ground in the last few pages and by now you will be itching to get at the paint box and to forget techniques for awhile. Much of your better work will be done from your accumulated notes in the privacy of your room or studio.

Perhaps you are one of those lucky ones who, when a moment of inspiration descends, can isolate yourself into a world of your own, produce your work of art while in a trance, emerging glowing and triumphant to the life of everyday matters. For most of us, it doesn't seem to work that way. Most professionals, accustomed to spending day after day at the job of painting, soon learn how to induce the "inspirational moment."

One of the chief difficulties, when working inside, is to make a start, to begin somewhere and then coax along the moment to grow out of itself into a number of exciting hours. Often it is a matter of facing a sheet of paper and preparing oneself by warming up with freely drawn scrawls or brush strokes the way a violinist will run a series of notes over the strings to loosen up his fingers. Another way is to look over your sketchbooks and notes. Many times a slight notation or hint of a composition will spark the imagination and provide the needed impetus.

Trying small paintings of a composition in one color or two, or varying the season in

which it was sketched, will often stimulate the imagination. Experiment by making a tracing of your sketch and reversing it. Sometimes this will improve your conception.

The snow painting shown here was done as a preliminary sketch. Using yellow ochre and ultramarine only, the tones and colors were varied by using dozens of combinations of mixtures; less water and one color; more water and two colors, two colors and little water, etc. Studies of this kind will often serve as preparations for livelier versions at a later time. The tight and self-conscious study allows you the luxury, later, of extracting only the essence of your theme. A similar way of working was shown in the still-life section, using jugs and bottles. After working your way through the more literal approach you will feel at home with the forms and will have considered the appearance sufficiently to be able to knock the facts about at will.

The large reproduction of the road and bay was the final version made from the felt-pen drawing. It was painted in much less time than the smaller watercolors reproduced here. Roughed in with charcoal and dusted off, on warm-tinted David Cox paper, it is a more successful interpretation of the subject than the preceding small studies.

Next time you are at a loss as to what to paint from your notes, try this system. Start somewhere, inspired or not. Once you are into the problem you'll gain momentum and your interest will quicken and grow.

THREE STEPS IN WATERCOLOR

Painting snow themes will be very helpful to you when you are beginning to paint in watercolor. It will provide a chance to use well-defined accents, plenty of white paper areas, and to use a simplified range of pigments. The colors suggested in the previous exercise—yellow ochre and ultramarine—will serve for this demonstration.

Here the drawing was put in with charcoal, dusted down to take off surplus charcoal, and then the washes applied directly and broadly.

A large, square-ended sable served to put in all the washes shown in this photograph. Notice the full saturation of the washes with pigment for the evergreen trees behind the house. Windows, and details are untouched at this stage.

When the washes were dry, details were put in with a smaller pointed sable. Ability to do a realistic handling of such subjects will provide training for the times when you go beyond the exercise stage to the inspired moments when idea, technique and execution seem to fuse and flow from the brush.

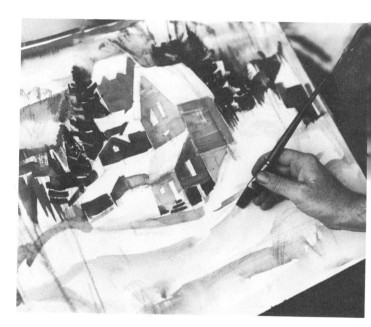

OUT OF DOORS

One of my early teachers, an old hand at sketching outdoors, liked to shock his students when he first accompanied them on sketching trips.

"The first thing to do," he would say, "is to look around for a comfortable, shady spot in which to sit. Then look around you for something interesting to paint."

He wasn't joking either, we discovered later. A shady place is essential to working, though some artists seem to invite difficulties. After you have sat half-blinded by the dazzling white paper reflecting the sun and sky, trying to judge tones of washes, or have seen on arriving home, your sketch change completely in its color and tone-values under a normal indoor light, you realize how important it is to paint under correct lighting.

There are times when it is impossible to find a convenient place, and there is nothing else to do but suffer and get something down fast. Normal sketching procedure *can* be organized, though more often than not, students handicap themselves with the wrong equipment, and then wonder why they get irritable or their work goes badly. I have listed in the Appendix the equipment which I have found most satisfactory. I have used and tested it from the snows of Canada to the tropics of the Pacific Ocean, assembling it after trying numerous variations of equipment.

Our experiments with limited colors yesterday will help us today. Silvery fog along the rocky shore, marsh grasses and the patterns of reflected trees in the small inlet will all come together into an ideal watercolor statement. Where do we begin, and how can we get some of it down before the fog lifts, the sun comes glaring into our eyes and the mood is no longer silver?

I suggest using plenty of water and your big brushes. Get the sky and water areas dropped in on a dampened surface first. Payne's gray warmed with a touch of ochre will give us the dark clouds. Lift off the medium-toned grays with a piece of cleansing tissue while the paper is wet, to get the soft edges of the cloud forms. Then the foreground areas, dropped in while wet, with ochre, sienna and umber. The reddish rocks in the middle distance can be modeled while the paper is damp. Use a smaller brush with almost dry color and let the line run slightly blending into the large washes. Now a few of the strong darks, using thalo blue and umber for the trees and their reflections. Luckily the air is heavy and damp and we have no trouble keeping our paper damp. Scratch out a few lines across the water to flatten it, and break up the reed areas with a few lines of texture.

Two ducks appear. Just what we need for an accent to give scale to our landscape. We use a smaller sable now and touch in the poles, tree branches, and accented lines of rocks and water's edge.

The fog lifts, the tones and colors change

and we're about finished. That great moment of standing back, lighting a cigarette, and seeing the results of our exciting labor, has come. Not bad, not bad at all. In fact, a good morning's work.

But the glow of satisfaction soon fades. That foreground should have been treated much more simply. Think what a Chinese master would have done with it! Maybe we we should try it over in the studio on a smoother-grained paper.

But it was worthwhile. At worst we've ruined a piece of paper and used up a little time. It's one more of that first five hundred watercolors ahead of us which are the hardest to do—and that's an achievement!

SOME LANDSCAPE PROBLEMS

SKIES

The experienced sketcher soon looks to his skies to set the mood of his landscape. He learns to know the quality of particular seasons and days and times of the day. Some days, why does everything seem to be overcast with a dominant blue color, or saturated with a pervading, curious, golden light? Is it, he asks himself, because the sky overhead has a peculiar ochre-pink flush which reflects everywhere, penetrating even the shadows? He notes too, on gray days, how the greens of the foliage seem to take on an extra richness, and how the sea and lake shifts and changes its color and tone with the movement of the sun through the sky.

To know the weather and to file away these varied moods for reference later in the studio when he can recall these particular qualities, is invaluable. I have always been intrigued by the notes scribbled on the sketches of such great landscape painters as Constable, Turner and Winslow Homer. A word or two recalls the day and the moment, even years later; "Sullen overhead," "mist and silver."

For the professional there is no such thing as the "perfect" day for sketching. It is only the amateur who will, on waking up on a dark morning to find it drizzling, decide he cannot do any painting that day. Some of the finest papers have been done when the clouds lie sodden, and mists lay a film of moving gray over the landscape.

It's not easy, naturally, to paint in bad weather. The practical considerations are worrisome. The paper lies wet and never seems to dry. (A chance here, though, to use some of that wet-in-wet technique we have been meaning to for a long time.) Rain spots may flick over our washes even though we find a sheltered spot in a doorway or arch. But even these nuisances can help at times. One damp morning I had almost finished a study of looming mountains, when it began to rain. I rushed the sketch to a finish when the first drops came down and ran to my car down the road. I discovered later that a corner of the water-color was spattered with minute white spots. Yet somehow, it helped the sketch, and gave a quality of "raininess".

While speaking of shelters, I would like to pass on a tip. It may seem obvious, but it is surprising how seldom it is used. When you are planning a sketching trip keep an eye open for hotels which have rooms with window vistas. Always look over the possibilities before you settle on the room you want, and choose the best view you can find. Many of my painter friends take advantage of this temporary studio arrangement. A useful book of hotels and inns where fine paintings have come into existence could be compiled. Figure sketches can be made without anyone suspecting. We know how the late Reginald Marsh used binoculars from his studio for hundreds of drawings of street figures. And if it does pour with rain, you have a ready-made shelter. And if subjects from the window are uninspiring—there are always clouds and skies.

amateurish than a broomstick tree which is not growing out of the ground, or daubs of green, meaningless strokes of paint.

None of these will solve the job for you but some may help if you yourself set out to *know* and *draw* trees constantly and seriously. If you love trees and want to paint them by all means get the book by John F. Carlson (Sterling). Mr. Carlson spent a lifetime learning to know trees and how to paint them. His chapter on trees in his book *The Elementary Principles of Landscape Painting* is excellent. *Trees and Landscapes* by Ted Kautzky is a helpful volume for the watercolor painter studying the technique of tree painting.

TREES AND FOLIAGE

One of the tests to give yourself from time to time to estimate your ability as a draftsman, watercolor painter and artist, is to paint a tree. Just an ordinary, run-of-the-mill, everyday tree. This is one of the most difficult of the forms nature sets out for us to paint, and unless you have developed your drawing abilities, your sense of design and form, the chances are that you will make a mess of it. Even after years of painting, it will be a challenge to you.

To really paint a tree, you should know it intimately; even *walk around it first*. You should know its character, how it differs from other trees, how it has its own laws of growth, and order of branching. Careful drawings such as those opposite will help your understanding.

Whether you draw it in green foliage or in winter, the problem is always there: How to take those thousands of twigs and leaves which so often seem to be nothing more than just a *blob* and develop from them forms and contours which are spirited and alive. It will require seeing and perception from you of a high order, and much patience. You must learn how to handle trees with some artistry, for you will constantly meet them as important parts of your sketching subjects. Nothing will make your work look more

NO. 12   5/8"

Strathmore Illustration
(Smooth)

Grumbacher
"Aquarelle"

Strathmore
"Students"

1.	2.	3.	4.	5.	6.	7.
Tinted Charcoal Paper	David Cox (English)	D'Arches (rough)	Whatman Handmade (medium rough)	Strathmore Student Watercolor	Grumbacher "Aquarelle"	Strathmore Illustration (smooth)

Whatman
Hand-made

David Cox
(English)

Tinted
Charcoal

BEACH AND SHORE

Tropical beach in the early morning with warm, brilliant light, the smash of the surf on the sand, debris and flotsam, jumping silver fish and boys net-fishing. Beautiful to see, yet as picture material flat and dull if we look at it through the camera lens. A photograph of a shoreline is most disappointing, the beach flattens out to a narrow strip and accurate perspective will give us something similar to the inset drawing. But it doesn't *feel* that way to us. Mentally, in the

mind's eye we feel the sensation, hear the thunder of the surf, the smash of water against the land, the movement of the rising sun, the spot and splatter of texture for miles along the beach.

So we paint it that way, tilting the planes up and toward the surface of the paper, a favorite device of the oriental artists. Long before the 15th Century and the discovery of basic perspective, the artist used this device. The further away an object is, the higher he puts it on his page, one plane behind the other. Study a Persian illumination and note how the walls and buildings are shown. Today we use this principle as "isometric perspective" in drafting blueprints and plans to show the construction of objects clearly.

Here we use it to obtain impact and a clearer definition of an experience.

(Below: actual size rendering of the type of exciting textures you will find on almost any beach.)

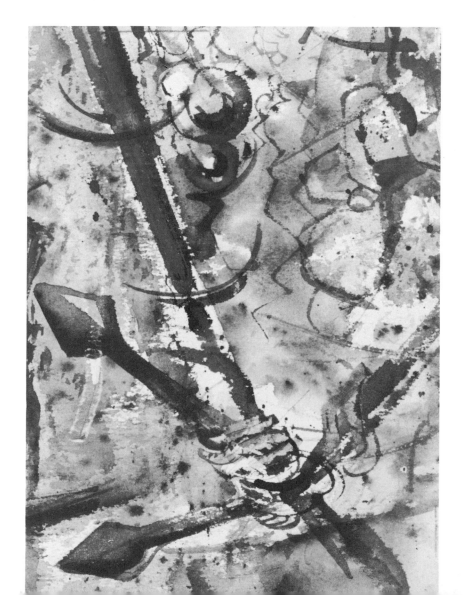

BEACH AND SHORE

Sand and Rocks; light ochre undertone first, cobalt and violet washes on top when dry. Warm rocks painted with burnt sienna and ultramarine.

The judgment of tone values is important. High-keyed sky, fainter middle distance and strongly saturated shadowed rocks in foreground.

Semi-dry brush work for broken strokes and sparkle of water. Note black ink pen line drawn in first before washes were applied.

Paper tinted first with light wash of ochre and blue to give an all-over glow of light. Umber, raw sienna and cobalt blue for warm grays.

Water; cerulean blue with touches of viridian green. Leave the white of the paper for surf. A detail from a larger sketch.

Reflections on wet sand. Drop color into wet paper without over-mixing colors in the pan. Paint dark rocks over this when dry.

WATERFALL

Cascading water and the deep green interior of the woods. A fine opportunity to practice some of the technical methods we have been demonstrating.

Painted on location at the base of a waterfall where the dank moss and rushing water made a chilly working spot for several hours. No trouble in keeping the paper wet for a wet-in-wet handling here.

The problem of sorting out the rocks and foliage into a meaningful design is a difficult one. A drawing or two will help establish the ground and rock forms over which the water flows. This will help to give a sense of solidity and form.

The rock just off center to the left was used as the pivot on which the rest of the shapes were drawn. The tree on the left was moved in from outside the picture to give a contrasting vertical foil against the movement of diagonals and broken shapes.

This sketch was painted on semi-smooth,

heavy paper with one flat brush and pointed sable. Large masses painted loosely first on sponged paper. Details gradually added as paper dried. Final water textures scraped in when paper was thoroughly dry.

Colors which were used: Thalo blue, thalo green, burnt umber, yellow ochre, Payne's gray and light red.

Some other techniques of handling water areas are shown in detail on Pages 98 and 99 "Beach and Shore" and in the next section on "Boats and Harbors."

BOATS IN HARBOR

A watercolor painted from sketch at top (opposite). When working later it was decided that the foreground did not hold enough interest. Shadow forms were strengthened in immediate foreground and the jetty brought forward at lower left-hand corner. Painted on smooth D'Arches paper, size one-quarter of full sheet, with a simple palette of ultramarine, yellow ochre, Payne's gray and viridian, with a few touches of bright color added last for flags and boats. This was painted in approximately one hour, including the drying of the sky, which was painted wet-into-wet.

BOATS IN HARBOR

Three felt-nib drawings done one morning on Nantucket Island. Actual size 10″ x 14″ in sketchbook. Ever-changing moods of sea and harbor require much study and observation before information can be put down in shorthand form. Notice simple indication of stormy sky which served to bring back tonal scheme of light water and dark sky in a watercolor done some months later.

FISHING SHEDS AND BOATS

Use the white paper areas to suggest high-keyed light. Learn to indicate detail by using only the essential forms. Make the flat ground areas lie flat by accenting horizontal strokes. Learn to eliminate and minimize unimportant data. Learn the construction of boats by drawing them in dry dock so that you will be able to make them look as though they are in the water, not sitting on top of it. Notice variety of dark and light strokes of pen made by controlling the amount of ink flowing from the felt-pen valve. The painting from this sketch is on page 49.

MORNING, ALVARADO, AND LIGHTHOUSE

Two paintings made on Strathmore semi-smooth illustration paper, using a full palette of colors. Color was lifted and sponged from paper in places. This is easy to do, as the color stays on the surface of illustration board without penetrating the paper deeply. Note dry brush used over washes, and wet-in-wet skies.

TROPIC BAY

Actual-size reproduction of a section of the inset watercolor to show how washes were applied on a smooth illustration board. Painted freely and rapidly, mostly wet-in-wet with detail subordinated to the general effect of afternoon light. Details put in with a Chinese brush when washes dried. Note razor blade strokes on hillside to suggest roofs.

1

2

106

PANORAMAS

There are times when a magnificent stretch of landscape is irresistible. The panoramas shown here were done out of doors, those opposite in watercolor, the one below in thin casein.

It is useful to search out a dominant accent which will serve as a pivot or point of interest for the receding planes of the vista, as well as giving a scale to help suggest the sweep of land by contrast. Place this accent well and let the rest of your forms be secondary to it, and you will have a chance at organizing what could easily become an "empty" subject.

In old-fashioned manuals on watercolor painting much attention was devoted to what was called "aerial perspective." This was an insistence on giving unlimited distance to the panorama by graying down the colors and lightening the tone values of objects receding into the distance. "Add more blue or gray, lighten the tone and soften the edges" was the formula.

Much of contemporary landscape painting shys away from such advice. It is in direct contradiction to the desire to make a controlled sense of space behind the picture plane, and to take from nature more than its purely visual aspect. Unlimited distances have a way of "knocking holes" in your composition. It is almost better to strengthen your lines and edges of distant objects, rather than have them dissolve into misty nothingness which does not function strongly with the rest of your composition. This is the weakness of sketch No. 1. The eye speeds across the mountains to the softened horizon, and on into infinity. No. 3 is a much stronger organization of a panoramic subject.

FIESTA

The skillful use of color dropped onto dampened paper is a favorite device exploited by watercolorists. It will take much practice to know how color spreads or bleeds, or how light it will be when dry. Try working with large masses first. As the paper dries, switch to smaller pointed brushes and pens to add final details which will dry with soft edges. Try picking up the color directly from the palette and paint it (without adding water) into the damp surface of the paper. An atomizer is useful in spraying and re-wetting areas which have dried too rapidly. Try various colored inks over large areas of underpainting. Constant experimenting will allow you to judge the amount of dampening necessary for different qualities of softness. Use a sponge or soak paper lightly in the sink before stretching on your board. Notice action lines of exploding fire-crackers and rockets and suggestion of crowded figures behind clown-band. "Mountain Landscape" frontispiece illustrates a good example of wet-in-wet technique.

WET ↘   DRY ↙

LIGHT
AND
DARK

PAINT WITH SMALL BRUSH INTO WET PAPER.

1. PENCIL OUTLINE AND
   WET PAPER
2. USE THICK PAINT
   ALMOST DRY BRUSH

" WET-IN-WET "

LIGHT

One of the many advantages for the sketcher who paints in watercolor, is the rapidity with which he can assemble his equipment, get to work, and put down, in a hurry if need be, a changing mood of nature. In the painting of light, the play of sun and shadow over out-of-door subjects, artists since the time of Turner have rejoiced in the watercolor medium as a means of catching fleeting impressions of nature.

The brilliant white surface of the paper is a good start, and we can modify it with glowing warm passages suggestive of the morning light or the last reflected side rays of afternoon light, working quickly using big brushes and plenty of water.

Try to feel, when you are painting rapid notes from changing landscape, the pervading light which sets the special mood of the moment. At times, even the shadows are filtered through with the pervading color, forming an allover harmony, which must be kept at all costs. Don't let small detail or local color distract you from keeping this unity of color. Eliminate ruthlessly any nonconforming color unless you are using it for purposes of contrast. Don't peer into the shadows too long as you paint. If you do, their values will lighten as your eye adjusts to the dark area. Judge the shadows in relation to the whole picture, not by themselves.

Study the edges of your forms carefully. Notice how the light will eat into them fraying their hard boundary lines. But remember at the same time how an overemphasis on "aerial perspective" and the softening of forms can easily lose your solidity and sense of structure. Notice how the silhouette of

poles and branches against the sky will lighten in value as the light creeps around them. You can avoid a "pasted-on" look if you remember that the pole will often appear *lighter* instead of darker by the contrast of the brilliant sky behind it.

Work quickly once you have chosen your subject, trying for the large effect. Leave it alone once the light begins to go and save the details until you are back in the studio, if need be. If you have trouble with the paper drying, when painting on location, especially on humid days, light a sheet or two of newspaper and hold the sketch over it—but make sure you are in a safe place while doing so. I remember too well the day I was about to do this when I suddenly realised I was painting on an anchored steel barge—filled with oil!

Judging the tone values of the relative light and dark passages will be one of your difficulties. Is the light bleached out all over? Is it dark, rich and low-keyed, as often happens on a wet humid day? Try and compare the subject with others you have done, in your mind, and pitch the key of tones accordingly. Study the sky carefully, for it will influence the landscape, changing the color and tone of water areas or distant mountains in a flash from dark and cold passages to warm light ones, as the light intensity changes.

Unless you study the changing moods of nature, your work as a landscape painter will suffer and will lack conviction and authenticity. If you are working in a semi-abstract way, you will need to know these moods even more intimately, for you are taking *only* the essentials and presenting them ungarnished.

Early morning. We are up long before

breakfast and out on the job. Already we have been thinking of the spot we want to paint. If it looked attractive in the midday glare when light is flat, the sun overhead and shadows lacking, how much more exciting it will be at seven o'clock!

No one is around to disturb us as we set out our equipment. This is the moment we have been waiting for and working towards. Now we will have our chance to use whatever we know of our profession. Do you feel the excitement of the moment? If you don't now, you never will.

You have not much to lose in sessions of this kind. A bit of paper, a little time, and the chances are that you will find yourself surprised with the freshness and merit of your sketch when you look at it the next day. You will have had little time to worry about technique. The controlled accident may have happened at the right place, for the necessity of putting down quickly and deftly the main elements will help even the timorous. There will be no opportunity to overwork the washes. The light will be gone too quickly for

that. The need for a rapid summing up and putting down essentials only will provide a useful impetus to your brush work.

Yet, if all goes wrong, don't let it discourage you. You cannot expect to produce a good thing every time. This is recognized by professionals who produce many works during a sketching week. There will be times when, in the nature of things, all goes wrong. There will be others when everything seems to fall into place. To give up, as some beginners do, after four or five sketches, is ridiculous. The professional watercolor painter realizes only too well how small the average of completely successful sketches can be.

So when your project ends up a mess—relax. Maybe the next time will be better, and I can guarantee that it will never become an easy matter of just sitting down to "dash off a fine watercolor." When you do produce a glowing, splendid paper you'll set a standard which will always be your aim. "Why can't I make this one come off well too?" you'll ask yourself, and look forward to the next opportunity to reach that level, and higher.

THE WASHING PLACE

Though reproduced without color, this painting will show you how watercolor lends itself to the depiction of shimmering light and shadow. "Juicy" fresh washes, strong light and dark patterns are a joy to paint. It is important that you use heavy paper which will not buckle into hillocks when soaked. Have plenty of pigment set out on your palette, use lots of water—and plunge in. Look, think, and feel the medium you are using. Know beforehand that a weak, timid sketch is inevitable unless you face the paper and brush with a strong determination to dominate them. But dilute this forceful approach with plenty of thinking *beforehand* and learn to call on the "delicate touch" when you need it. Watch those last accents and calligraphic strokes. If they add nothing—leave them out.

Looking into morning light provides strong contrasts. Keep high values of white paper and use strong wet-in-wet darks. Observe how the light eats into the edges of objects, such as roof tops, masts, and distant mountains.

1

TOWARD ABSTRACTION — *AN EXPERIMENT*

This is a story about a cactus plant, but it could easily have been about a person, an animal or a group of houses.

I am relating it here, where space is limited, because it is a way of demonstrating to you at one time most of the things we have been writing about; subject matter, composition, orchestration, the over-all conception, and how the use of synthesis and imagination can lift your work from mediocrity.

I had been discussing these things one morning with York Wilson, Canadian artist, and we had become deep in painters' talk, the problem of how to carry through from fac-

tual material to meaningful creative work. It was at that moment that we decided that if we were any kind of artists at all, we should be able to take the least promising material, and by using whatever perception and knowledge we had, be able to produce a worth-while picture after we had generated sufficient creative impetus. It would depend upon what we *did* with the material presented to us.

Our experiment followed. We decided to drive out into the country, stop the car at a mileage point decided upon previously, and instead of picking our spot, limit ourselves

2

to whatever faced us at the right-hand side of the road. This would prevent us from choosing a favorite subject or one whose problems we knew we could solve easily.

We stopped on the dot of mileage 14,286.04 and found ourselves staring at a desolate, dried field with three cactus plants as large as small trees, and a stone wall.

"Quite inspiring," muttered Wilson to himself, while I tried to look nonchalant and unperturbed by the desolation.

We spent most of the morning staring, turning over rocks, walking around the green, spiky plants, and trying to visualize what

could be made from such unlikely beginnings. If a painter had to be in love with his subject to do anything worthwhile, we would have been finished.

We had agreed that after we had made our notes, absorbed our material, we would have two weeks in which to complete our paintings. Then we would meet and exchange notes on our productions. Wilson made some careful drawings of cactus forms and I finally, in desperation, did a literal watercolor, putting in everything I could see for future reference. It is reproduced here as No. 1.

We drove back to our studios feeling rather

The reproduction of "Sun and Cactus" on page 118 was done on a soft velvety Chinese rice paper. Painted with yellow tint and gray, plus a pen line of brown ink, it was done as directly as possible, without overworking. This paper is as fragile as a butterfly's wing and must be handled as delicately or the paper will tear while wet. The luminosity and glow of a successful painting on such paper justifies the difficulties of using it.

YORK WILSON

foolish and thinking that we could have at least picked a more intriguing mileage with potential picture-making material.

A few of the results of that morning are reproduced throughout this book. I wish I could show you all of Wilson's set of twelve large studies and paintings which evolved from many weeks of work afterwards, based on this unpromising theme. The fact that we had to make something from so little became a challenge to us, and we found ourselves exploring every inch of it, extracting an element here, a sensation there. Our imagination was called into play as we found ourselves making different versions of the theme.

You will understand some of the thinking processes this brought about. What was the important matter we wanted to convey in terms of paint using design and color? The spirit of the desolate land? Growth, with the

light blazing down through the varied cactus forms, moving and shifting, revealing textures? Or a combination of things? As we worked, the subject itself became less and less important. We took what we wanted and left the rest.

Number 2 was painted in scarlet, grays and black, eliminating the natural greens and concentrating on an integrated all-over design which would give the mood of Mexican earth. It is one of the strongest of my sketches, I feel.

Number 3 took a section of plant form and tried to show the curious, stark growth reaching to the sky, the movement of light in and about the spiky clumps. The color was based on a gray-green-orange scheme, and many hours were spent building up textures.

Number 4 on Page 120 is the final painting which came about after many hours of painting cactus themes. It is in black and white with touches of yellow. Almost all literal shapes are discarded; the subject, as such, has almost disappeared. The painting itself of moving forms of light and dark is a conclusion which was hinted at in painting Number 3. Shapes, forms, textures have grown into a unit far beyond the first visual impact of that first morning. Yet without this impact, this final interpretation would not have come into being. This painting is in the permanent collection of Carpenter Galleries, Dartmouth College, Hanover, New Hampshire, and if you should see it there you will know how and why it was painted.

Perhaps our experiment will suggest a way out for you when you feel you have run out of ideas or material for your painting. Places you often passed may have great possibilities —perhaps you have been planning for some time to do something with them—why not try them soon, using *your* interpretation?

3

4

THE BONES OF A LANDSCAPE

Here is another experiment for you to try. Next time you are travelling by car or train, perhaps on business or merely for pleasure, make a concentrated effort to study the landscape and character of the country through which you are passing. Let it filter through your mind clearly, impressing your memory with its essential forms and contours. Check it against other landscapes you have seen. What are its comparative differences? Does it lie flat, or roll? What are its special qualities and rhythms? How does the color compare with other parts of the country? Does it feel lusher or dryer, is it richer or more desolate? Make a conscious effort to sort out all these impressions and file them away in your mind.

When you are back in your hotel or room, take a piece of paper and your watercolors, and while these impressions are still with you, before new sights pour in on you, endeavor to put down something about that day's experiences. Recall the large qualities, not details or individual memories of just one spot. Was the day *heavy*? Try and put down the heaviness. Do you remember mostly a sensation of jagged lines or of swinging curved rhythms? Put them down. Don't worry about accuracy or literal drawing. Recollect a synthesis of all the sights and feelings. There will be an overlapping of many things. Put some of them down without regard to your photographic memory: "There seemed to be many houses. There were miles of black woods stark against the early evening sky. Roads crossed over the hills in every direction."

If you practice this you will be surprised how soon you will cultivate your memory to bring away with you the *bones* of a landscape. After several attempts this will become easier. You will begin to look for the structural patterns under the many visual sensations you experience in a day.

Let yourself be free in this experiment and don't be afraid of ending up with a strange-looking picture. You are trying to teach yourself how to pierce through millions of facts to symbols of reality. Training yourself in this way will aid you to go more directly to the substance of your vision. Look for the backbone of your landscape underneath the detail.

THE IMAGINATIVE CONCEPT

We have, I hope, come some distance in our thinking since reading the first pages of this book. We have stressed the necessity for having some skill in representation, and the need for having a vocabulary with which to work. Beyond this, we have tried to bring to your attention the more important facets of the watercolor challenge, the need for exercising the imagination to provide fresh concepts and ideas, along with the development of the artist's eye.

In these last pages I have selected a snow theme to illustrate how we have moved on from the kind of painting and thinking we used in the exercise on page 87. There we clung rigidly to the traditional idea of a watercolor subject, depicting the facts more or less photographically. The ground planes are visually correct, the houses drawn in correct perspective—a routine, if fairly skillful manipulation of washes and colors. After years of painting out of doors, this can be

done almost to recipe, unless the artist seeks to develop by delving into more complex ways of expressing deeper qualities.

In other words, this one is a repetition of problems which have been solved long ago by others. As an exercise in technique it may have some value; as a picture it is rather dull and commonplace in conception.

On page 123 there is a better effort. It has more vitality, both in its idea and presentation. The aim was to give the feeling of frosty northern night when the air seems to shift in cold bands and the stars come down to join the sparkling snow banks. In it I tried to conjure up the *feeling* of many such nights, of no one place or time. It was painted from memory in a nostalgic moment. I had been listening to the magnificent music of Vivaldi's "The Seasons," and the winter theme became so haunting that I had to try the mood.

You will notice that the planes are not *visually* accurate. Areas move and cross each other, the music of black and white rhythms are dominant. The forms of trees and bushes are symbolized and simplified. A decorative use of line and mass has been used. Yet the picture must get beyond the formalities of design. We are not making a Christmas card,

though there is no reason why the painting could not be used for one—after it has been conceived. Perhaps you will see why I consider this a stronger statement, containing more feeling of "winteriness" than page 87.

On this page is another experiment which followed on the second painting. Here the facts of house, trees, sky and snow have been discarded altogether. The rhythms and color scheme of cold blues, grays and yellows have been kept. There may be a hint of winter forms, if you look for them—icicle shapes or stormy cloud forms, but this was not intentional. All that remains is a "painting." It differs from others in this book because it does not depend upon visual subject matter or communicate through recognizable forms. It—the color, the movement of shape and counter-shape, the textures of the paint itself, and the over-all design provide the reason for its being—not the subject in it.

We are in deep waters here. Perhaps you do not comprehend or cannot react to pictures which lack realistic forms on which to lean. Such pictures may bewilder you. You may even get angry and want to have long discussions about the "lack of communication" or a "too personal language" which means nothing to anyone but the artist. They may do nothing more for you than give you the same sensation as looking at a nicely-textured and colored piece of fabric. If you feel this way, don't pretend otherwise. But don't close in on your searching and thinking, to dismiss the nonfigurative painting as nonsense or meaningless. You will be cheating yourself if you do. Think of it as only one more way of working, and that when it is done from an inner necessity to sincerely express the artist's feelings, a most compulsive and difficult way. You will discover this for yourself as you work and study and someday feel impelled to strike out toward the new languages and freedoms of contemporary painting.

THE TECHNIQUE OF CASEIN

CASEIN TEXTURES

There seems little advantage in painting in casein unless you are able to add new qualities and textures to your work which you cannot obtain by using other opaque media such as gouache, tempera, etc. It is a comparatively expensive pigment and can be easily wasted through drying up on the palette. Casein brush strokes dry rapidly, generally to a lighter tone than they appear when wet. Darks are hard to preserve and the newcomer to casein will be bewildered by the difficulties of matching colors and of avoiding a certain chalkiness in his finished pictures.

It is a fallacy too, that casein can be used transparently and will appear as fresh and transparent as pure watercolor, and when a painter tells me he uses casein so that "you can't tell the difference from an oil-painting" it seems rather pointless to me. What then, are the advantages to using casein? It is only a few years since it became readily available in tubes in art stores, and since then, its popularity has grown enormously. You will find caseins in most exhibitions, so much so that a new National Casein Society has just been formed for the sole purpose of exhibiting caseins. What are its essential qualities and why does it appeal to contemporary painters?

The most important quality to me is the number of rich textural possibilities it provides. Once you have learned to control the medium you may indulge a love of detail and textures *ad infinitum*. Its capacity for drying fast becomes an asset which can be invaluable. Instead of waiting for an undercoating of thick pigment to dry—generally a matter of days with regular oil-paint—you can build up a surface with broken textures, impastos of thick paint, and the pigment will be hard enough to apply thin glazes or overpaintings of transparent color in an hour or two. Another appealing quality which is its alone, is the beautiful mat surface—a velvety bloom of the pigment itself which is not to be found in any other paint. It comes from the binding agent, a milk derivative, which seems to hold the powdered colors in a clean and appealing suspension. Perhaps the quick drying has something to do with it or the fact that it is an emulsion of water and oil; whatever it is you will seldom get those sour and muddy colors so easily obtained with mixtures of oil paint and oil. Even the neutral grays and off-browns retain their clean luminosity.

To use the medium well there are certain limitations to be observed. It is not wise to apply the paint directly with a palette knife as it comes from the tube. Some dilution with water in the brush will avoid the possibility of thick pigment cracking when dry. A satisfactory dilution is to dip the brush in water and give the paint on the palette a stir to bring the casein to a consistency of thick cream. This can be piled up in layers, one over the other to a considerable thickness, if required. Scraping down layers of semi-dry and very dry pigment is also a useful procedure which will give broken and scintillating color areas.

Most newcomers to casein try one or two experiments and give up. They use the pigment as though they are painting with poster color, brushing in flat areas. The result is a washed-out texture which could have been obtained just as easily with any opaque paint. They do not realize that casein becomes enriched, its brushwork varied and surfaces more appealing, if it is worked over and into. By using stiff bristle brushes and applying the paint with scrubbed-in strokes, the forms can be modelled with variations of edges and assorted thicknesses of paint in countless ways. By using the end of the brush to mould the thick paint when it is semi-wet and by using a razor blade, new manipulations and exciting treatments will suggest themselves.

The reproduction heading this section shows some of the ways casein may be used. Some of the mixed techniques which combine wax crayons, transparent overlays of color, and various uses of varnishes and emulsions are demonstrated in the following pages. A list of necessary equipment to add to your watercolor gear is given in the appendix.

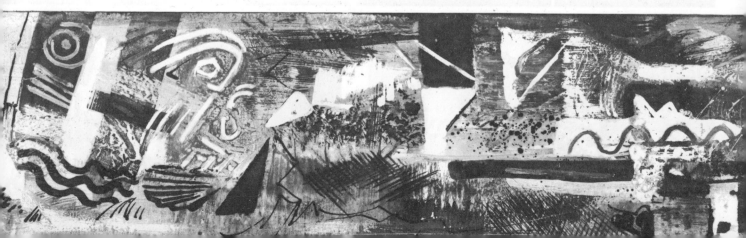

2   1   3

CASEIN GLAZE TECHNIQUE

In contrast to painting directly with colored opaque casein is the method shown here. It is a variation of the Old Master principle of tonal underpainting and oil glazes. Its purpose is to give a richness to the color by overlaying thin transparent washes of watercolor over a painting done in a one-color underpainting. By this method of working the composition, textures and drawing problems are all solved *before* the addition of color.

Begin with plenty of water and black, or if you choose, a neutralized blue or warm grey. (I find a mixture of light red and ultramarine a sympathetic underpainting color; early painters preferred a gray-green *imprimatura*, especially for figure subjects.) Paint loosely, blocking out the large shapes in a manner shown in the first step on page 130. Gradually build up to thicker pigment and add white paint to your color.

If you leave this overnight and then isolate the painting with a thin brushing over with a soft sable brush using Shiva Ethereal Varnish, the painting will be ready for glazing. The glaze used here was simply water and a selection of the most transparent colors in the watercolor box. Occasionally I have found the brilliant staining dye colors such as Schminke watercolors invaluable for glazes, but it is wise to make a test for permanence, and to avoid the overgarish mauves and pinks. Washes are applied over the underpainting, several applications being applied until the richness of color is achieved. You will find it useful to keep the underpainting lighter in value than it will be finally, as the glazes will naturally lower the tone.

At the last opaque casein was used here and there to touch up the high values on the snow. A final coat of Ethereal varnish was applied several days later. A high-gloss varnish was avoided. (See Appendix for the properties of varnishes).

Inset are several useful techniques to use with casein.

1. Thin semi-opaque glazes of warm transparent undertone. This thin painting allows drawing over with pen lines and ink. This is difficult to do over thick paint, besides the danger of peeling and flaking of the ink later.

2. A yellow transparent glaze over warm thick casein texture which was built up first with a rubber roller and palette knife. (See Architectural Subjects on page 136 where this technique is invaluable).

3. Opaque touches of casein used over a transparent watercolor painting. This is a mixed technique which is frowned upon by watercolor purists but is a legitimate manner of working if not used as a constant patch-up device for watercolor failures. The flower sketch on page 62 was done in this way.

All three reproductions are the same size as the originals.

If you wish to try the casein-oil technique, the following is recommended by Ramon Shiva. Let the casein painting dry for at least two hours. Apply a thin coating of Ethereal varnish. Mix ordinary oil colors to the desired color hue and reduce the color with Glazing varnish and apply thinly. Allow a period of at least twelve hours for the oil colors and Glazing varnish to set before again painting with casein. Glazes may be wiped off for correctional purposes if done immediately with a cloth damp with turpentine. Casein can then be painted back into the picture and when thoroughly dry a final coat of varnish applied, though this is very tricky and unless sprayed on or brushed lightly, can disturb the glazes.

Many oil painters, avoiding the complications of the above technique, use the advantages of quick-drying Shiva Underpainting White (a casein-oil white) to build up their textures, instead of the regular white oil paint. Over this they use their oils in the usual fashion.

FIRST STEP: *Over light pencil, transparent washes of thinned casein or watercolor are washed in to establish the main values of light and dark. Use a neutral gray-blue or grayed warm tint made with ultramarine and a touch of light red. No attempt is made to finish detail, although textures can be indicated for further development in opaque color later.*

This photograph of the subject was taken in a Nova Scotia fishing village. For a casein study it has a good variety of textures; shingles, grassy foreground, nets and shimmering water. The strong light-and-dark pattern lends itself to strong pattern making, though the dark area in the large fishing shed is too heavy in the snapshot.

THREE STEPS IN PAINTING IN CASEIN

SECOND STEP: *Large areas of casein scrubbed in with a bristle brush over washes. Paint should be slightly diluted with water, but brush strokes can follow forms and indicate textures in various layers and thicknesses. Keep values to main darks, white and one or two intermediate tones. Remember light areas can be glazed over with transparent washes of casein later.*

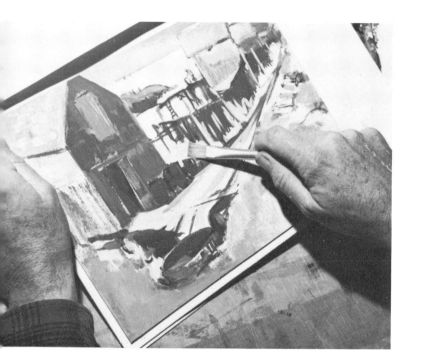

THIRD STEP: *Forms built up and emphasized with small strokes of a pointed sable brush over underpainting. Crosshatching, scumbling casein over rough underlayers of paint strokes, scraping down with razor blade—all of these means can be used to mould the paint. If pigment goes dead from too much overworking, a thin coat of Ethereal varnish (Shiva) will bring up darks. There is also an emulsion which can be added to the pigment when thinning it down with water which gives it added covering power. This exercise was painted entirely in black and white casein.*

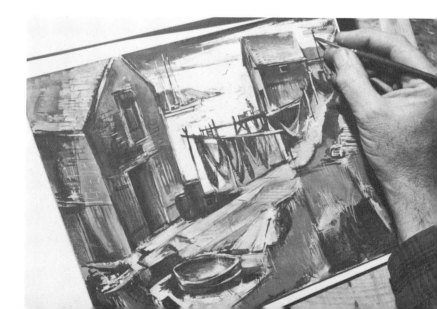

FULL-COLOR CASEIN

The method of working in full color is similar to the way shown in the tonal demonstration previously. I like to set out a number of colors I expect to use on a white enamel butcher's tray, squeezing out a fair-sized gob of paint from the tube (at least an inch).

The transparent wash goes on as in the photograph, (Step One, page 130) but this is often varied in color. If the sketch is to be of a *warm* scheme, I often keep the undertone in a *cooler* tone, more blue than light red. This is allowed to come through at times and gives a vibration and liveliness to the paint, especially if it is a thinly painted casein.

Having decided on the mood I wanted to paint, I tried to visualize the color scheme before I began, reducing the large areas to their simplest main color. This was to be in a low key, grays set against a warm foreground, a note of red dominating the sheds, and the glitter of light on the water reflecting a break in the sky. The sense of movement worked out in the black and white sketch was to be kept, but any changes I felt like making as the color was built up would be made without worrying about the first planned design. Additions of detail to break up dull spaces were made, a net on the left instead of the shadows of the boards, some floats on the right to pick up a light accent in a dark corner.

Painted in several afternoons in the studio, the paint was allowed to build up, layer after layer, for textural quality. When it became too thick, or deadened from over-working, it was sprayed with Ethereal varnish very lightly, and when dry, worked on again. Here and there it was scraped down with a razor blade revealing underneath colors. If the sketch begins to look too worked over and finicky, a large brush and broad scumbles of paint will soon bring back a broader treatment. Final details were put in last with a small brush and well-thinned paint. Be sure and rinse brushes constantly or use clean ones, as the colors will pick up the remains of white or high-keyed color in the brush, giving every area a chalky, unpleasant appearance.

Don't be afraid of putting work into your caseins. If your picture gets out of hand, set it aside for a few days and come back to it with

a fresh eye. You will often see what is wrong with it at the first return glance. If it gets beyond all saving (and don't give up too soon) don't tear it up. I put aside my failures and when I am through the day's work at casein painting, I take the remaining scraps of color on my tray and scrub them into these failures, or on to fresh boards. These are put away to dry thoroughly and I often use them for textured bases on which to paint other compositions. Scraped down to underlaying paint or sanded, colors will come through which may at times be incorporated in a final picture. When stuck for an inspiration, the rich color and abstract brushstrokes will often start an idea growing.

CASEIN PAINTINGS

TONE VALUES IN CASEIN

Even when you are concentrating on painting in full color, do not neglect to consider carefully the tonal pattern of light and dark values. This is one of the weaknesses of the beginner in casein. The colors will dry *lighter* than they appear when they are wet and it will take practice to be able to judge this difference. Overmixing of the color, especially the darks, or dirty brushes and water, will also lighten values so that the chalky appearance we have mentioned before will impregnate all colors. *Keep the darks clean.* Isolate lighter underpainting with Shiva Ethereal varnish before painting over your darkest notes, and you will have no trouble.

See to it that you have a well-planned pattern of tonal values before you begin painting in color. The massing of these, the areas which will hold and attract the most attention, are vital to your composition.

In the spot sketch of the nets and harbour, the darkest notes were placed next to the light values in the cluster of houses. Even the sky glow was subdued to this point of interest. This provided a focal point on which the eye could settle.

The deserted silver mine forms were worked out from drawings and studies made on the spot. Textures were built up with layers of casein, pen lines, and thin transparent glazes. Here the light value of the foremost arches was used as a resting point in contrast to the broken textures of wall and debris.

Both in value (the lightest light) and in the unbroken texture of the white wall, this area dominates the composition. The rest of the forms work around and in relation to it. Notice the small cross on the hill and how important it is to break the movement of the strong diagonal mountain line.

ARCHITECTURAL SUBJECTS

Casein is ideally suited for renderings of textures in buildings, especially broken walls, adobe and stone.

It is not an easy medium to use out of doors, lending itself more conveniently to working in the studio. When working with it on the spot I have found it important to have plenty of water available—much more than for watercolor. The pigment saturates the water jar, brushes need cleaning more often to avoid chalkiness in the dark colors, and it is hardly possible to build up glazes, scrapings and textural qualities in one sitting. I prefer to sketch in pencil, rough-in transparent washes as shown in the demonstra-

tion plate on Page 130, and work the casein over this in the studio.

Another disadvantage is that the colors dry rapidly outside, especially in hot summer weather and much waste occurs as the colors harden. However there are times when the subject calls for a casein rendering on location and it can be done. The reproduction of a deserted town was done in one painting on location with direct semi-thick pigment with very little manipulation over the basic lay-in of casein. Painted in a warm key of pinks, ochres and dusty umbers on a semi-rough watercolor paper, it is a good example of the direct casein technique.

TANNERY RUINS

Thinly painted with casein on David Cox paper. Varied textures of old stone walls were achieved by allowing transparent watercolor areas to show through the opaque casein touches here and there. A fine brush and pen-line was used to strengthen the drawing, tying together the strong black-and-white pattern of shadowed arches and ruined walls. A few thin transparent glazes were painted over the painting at the very last, especially in the right-hand top-corner and immediate foreground areas to enrich the color where it had gone dead from too much over-painting.

137

A studio picture from drawings and sketches. Here the devices of mixing media were exploited to the fullest. Thin washes, pen and ink, glazes, splatterings and scraping through to underlayers were used to obtain the feeling of age-old ruined buildings. A very limited color scheme helped to set the somber mood. A blue sky, which was there when the sketches were made, was rejected and a brooding storm was put in consistency of mood, so that everything would add up to one impact; color, design, technique.

A painting of this kind can stand all the work you care to put into it. Initially, it was a jotting similar to the drawing heading page 136—a two-minute structural analysis.

ORANGE SELLERS

The difficulty of integrating sky areas with other parts of the picture was noted on page 78. In this casein, the problem was to make the sky planes function against the architectural domes and buildings. If you imagine this sky left blank, you can see how the agitated strong forms of black and white would need related tonal areas in the upper part of the picture. By playing light forms against dark edges and dark edges against light, plus building up the right-hand corner of the sky with strong directional lines, an allover unity is made.

Painted in one session in tones of orange, gray and warm pink-ochre, without glazes or much overpainting.

This was made on a full sheet of smooth illustration board. Painted from notes and memory of a pile-up of houses in Guanajuato, a wonderful silver-mining town on the Mexican plateau which is a painter's paradise.

The houses, building up the steep hillside, make almost cubist compositions without changing radically the facts of perspective or reality. I have done numerous watercolors of this theme and always the visual excitement of the vertical and blocked out forms against the curved lines of washing hung out to dry, the spotting of doorways and windows on the large flat walls, leaves me believing I am looking at a stage set.

A limited color scheme was used here: Umber, black and white with some yellow notes. Concentration was on the design and pattern made by these cave-dwellers' homes where stout hearts and steep climbs are the order of the day.

By turning the picture upside down you will get a better idea of its structural and abstract basis. Forget that they are houses and see the pattern of light and dark areas as forms only. Notice how the placing of the spots of doors and windows has been planned. Without this, the maze of detail would end up in a hodgepodge of conflicting accents. Black on white, white on black, the changes are made when the area calls for an accent to relieve a dead passage or area. The one large house, at the bottom of the page where the steps lead upwards, is the anchor on which the lesser areas depend. Without this open space of light, the whole scheme would collapse from too much busyness. Without color, in the limitations of black and white, it has a tendency to do this. In color, sections of yellow and yellow-gray help to support the leading of the eye from area to area and to provide a visual resting place at intervals. The washing on the line plays its part in this way, repeating colored walls elsewhere.

The diagram will give you the skeleton plan which appealed to me when I glimpsed the subject from a hotel window. Relative shapes were changed, the vertical upsweep of the walls and houses was emphasized.

The two suggested figures at the bottom of the picture were put in, taken out, and put in again. Were they necessary to give scale or did they destroy the almost unreal, mysterious houses? Finally they were left in, but brought to simplified nonobtrusive forms which would merge into the black and white pattern. Cover them with your finger and see if you would have left them in or have taken them out.

THE LITTLE CHAPEL

A complicated subject painted more or less as is. Here the forms in themselves are so varied that there was little need to change the visual facts. Certain adjustments had to be made, windows left out, others put in. Sizes of towers and domes were modified to avoid monotony. Colorful washing on the line, a rooster and hen to break up the front blank wall and the dark note of an orange tree brought into the left-hand corner. A rainy season sky for a backdrop provided a contrast for the sunlit ancient buildings.

Such subjects require patience and forethought in planning. The careful placing of accents and shadow forms is imperative to avoid spottiness of too many details.

This painting was made from a note similar to the inset drawing. I often wonder if the owner, somewhere in California, has noticed the question-mark motif, the structural line pattern of the picture. It was the only note I could make at the time in the hushed sanctuary of the shrine.

Glitter of candles, electric lights around the altar and the glint of gold and silver. All of these were built up the next day with casein which is admirable for obtaining such effects. Painted with transparent color first on a rough watercolor paper, the candle flames and glowing circles of light were put in at the very last.

143

SEA AND ROCKS

The dynamic forms of sea-battered rocky coast set against the late afternoon sun is the theme of this casein picture. Overlapping planes of foreground and middle-distance are tied together by emphasizing the large diagonal structural areas. Over these basic shapes, textures have been developed using broken edges, hard edges and lines to orchestrate separate elements of the composition.

The glare of the sun on the water, the fishing boats, clouds, etc. have been simplified to symbols, leaving out all unnecessary details.

The right-hand side of the composition clearly shows how the background shapes have been tied up with the immediate foreground, in other words, our old problem of "respecting the flatness of the picture-plane."

The picture was painted on smooth illustration board. It was started on the spot with the pattern washed in with transparent washes. Finished later, in the studio, its color scheme is based on dark umbers and browns, with a harmony of orange and related warm colors to tie it together.

Notice how textures are varied. Large bristle brushes were used to rough in the large areas, and small sables used to write in the finer line details of bushes, boats, etc.

ONE RING CIRCUS (See Page 19)

Paintings of this kind are exciting to do, and give some idea of the brilliance of color possible with casein paint.

Don't be afraid to try this kind of subject if it appeals to you. The sketch reproduced on page 19 involves another technical device which may be of value to you. To obtain the all-over background of broken blacks and night feeling, the paper was first roughed out with casein, semi-thick, with no regard for details. When this was dry a wide bristle brush was used to paint over everything lightly with black India ink. When this was dry, the paper was rinsed under the tap and scrubbed lightly with a soft brush. Much of the ink was removed in this way, allowing the casein color to come through here and there. This was used as an *imprimatura* or undercoating on which the painting was then developed when thoroughly dried, and a thin spray of Ethereal varnish used. Details were built up over the large areas, but here and there the mottled passages of black and casein were left to suggest the crowds in the depth of the sagging tent. Most of the detail was concentrated on the chief actors in the ring, and the rest left sketchy and lost in the off-stage and overhead.

The amount of detail possible can be gauged by noticing the highlight on the clown's bulbous nose. Small brushes were used for these final touches.

Size of illustration paper 16″ x 20″. Full range of colors used with brushes scaling from large bristle to finest sable.

The above technique may be useful to you if you wish to try involved subjects with crowds, parades, skating rinks, etc., especially in strong contrasting night-lighting.

GRAPES (See Page 40)

This subject may not seem very exciting as such, yet when we learn to explore the assembly of facts with new eyes, looking for structure, relationship of planes, selecting a color scheme to bring it to life, the possibilities are unending.

Technical data on this painting will give you a clue to the mixtures possible to obtain the richness of a fully developed casein.

First , wax crayon, yellow, white and brown. These strokes to break up large areas later in the process of painting, by scraping through to the wax. Then transparent watercolor glazes in neutral tint to establish drawing and design. Casein was then painted in thin layers with not too much impasto and transparent glazes of mauve glazed over lighter casein-painted grapes. The blacks were scrubbed-in thinly with a clean brush. Note pattern of bowl broken into planes to avoid monotony of symmetrical shape in center of picture.

The painting proceeds by painting into and over with opaque and glazed touches, each part growing, and background shapes changing to relate to objects. Each part must function with the other.

Someone once said: "You start the picture, but it finishes itself." If you understand this, you will have no worry about when to leave off working, or knowing when the picture is *complete*.

FIREWORKS AND NIGHT EFFECTS

The plate *Night Fiesta* is taken from a published portfolio of twelve colored reproductions of paintings of the Mexican Christmas *Posadas*.

Made a few years ago from rough notes sketched in at night as the parades took place, the pictures were painted the following morning while memory of color was fresh in the mind. The series demonstrates the useful qualities and brilliance of casein in interpreting sparkle of flares, glow of lanterns, and the bursting parabolas of skyrockets.

You may not have such material handy, but similar color effects can be found in any modern American city where the neon light turns drab corners into a paintable fairyland. Tinted papers are useful as a base to work on, or watercolor paper may be colored beforehand to a desired hue which is left as a background color for night effects.

SUMMING UP

Throughout this book I have tried to show you how close is the bond between technique and the creative concept, between the thinking and the execution. The one grows out of the other. The first alone, with hard work and practice, will produce clever and skilled technical performances; the second alone will produce cerebral exercises communicating little of genuine creative intensity. The union of the two is always evident in a work of art.

I have tried to demonstrate my conviction that an intelligent and objective analysis of what we are trying to accomplish with paint and brush, will help us to strike out beyond a dull and literal response to the live world of true creativity. The illustrations used here have been reproduced with the admonition that none of them pretends to be *your* solution of the problems uncovered. They are one man's way, which should suggest others to you, as they always do to the painter himself, when he has done his utmost and can't wait to try once again.

The growth and transition to new ways of working occurs in cycles. Periods of lassitude while new sensations are being absorbed, blind alleys down which the artist stumbles, moments of enlightenment and supreme conviction of the rightness of his approach—all of these coalesce and from time to time produce good results. When this happens, it is a fine moment indeed. It balances the moments of dejection and weeks of trivial productivity which must occur to every man who devotes his lifetime to painting.

As a parting word for those who need encouragement, and a helpful push in low-spirited moments, I pass along a sentence I discovered in G. B. Shaw's writings. It should, more than any words I could write, provide the reassurance you may be looking for.

"I look," he writes, "to the provincial and the amateur for genuine fecundity in art."

What more could you want?

A corner of this kind, where all necessary equipment is right at hand, is invaluable for working inside. Papers, colors, brushes and sketchbooks; rubber-cement and varnishes; everything is within easy reach for those hectic moments when color and water flies through the air. The desk (a modified kitchen cabinet) has a slightly sloping top of about 15 degrees and is high enough to work at when standing up. A long table for cutting mounts (not shown in the photograph) is a valuable addition.

APPENDIX

It is important always to buy the best quality materials. The practical job of providing ourselves with the proper equipment for our work seems a simple enough matter. Yet I have never begun instructing a class in which every individual appeared completely and comfortably outfitted for the job ahead of him. In many cases the students seemed to have gone out of their way to handicap themselves in the way of materials and equipment — as though they didn't have enough to contend with in the actual problems of painting!

It is easy enough to say that a real artist doesn't have to be concerned with such matters; he could dash off a masterpiece with a child's fifteen cent box of paints and a cat's-hair brush. (I have yet to see such a work of art.) If there is such a masterpiece around, we can be sure that the addition of good paper, unfading colors and cleaner brush work would not do it any harm.

In any case, the least we can do for ourselves is to see that our equipment will help rather than hinder us, especially if we are in the beginning stage. So often the faults of a badly planned sketching kit are so obvious that one feels foolish to point them out. But because of their importance in watercolor painting, which is in some ways like performing a clean, deft operation, we give here a careful check-list of materials which might be of service, even to the professional.

Have we, for example, tried out some of those new colors we've had our eye on for some time, colors we've never tried, all the Thalo series, or Mars colors? Are we still using the same old grade of paper, the same texture and weight as always, or would it be of value to branch out and

try some other brand just to see what might happen? Does our sketching easel really serve us the way we want it to, or would it be a good idea to investigate new types which have come on the market recently? Not many of us like changing our habits, but there's nothing like occasionally breaking loose from our set ways. It's so easy to fall right back into them.

Let's begin our list with one of the more essential items of our painting gear, the paint box.

Over the years, I have tried many variations and sizes of boxes, beginning with the proud ownership of my Christmas gift child's box and ending up with a rather too-complicated custom-built one I designed myself and had made by a local tinsmith. Recently I came upon one of the most practical and workable boxes of all, and it has become my favorite. It is a large, simple watercolor box (11″ x 14″ when the two halves are open). It is light, has plenty of room for mixing washes and has a thumb hole for holding the box when I am working out of doors, plus a detachable cup for water which I seldom use, preferring my larger army cup and water canteen.

There is no standard name for this box, but when it came on the market from somewhere in Germany, it was immediately sold out. Its chief feature which artists like is the roomy partitions for color to be squeezed into. One partition will hold more than a full tube of watercolor and there are fourteen divisions for a full choice of colors. Looking at these big, fresh gobs of paint will free even the most timid student from delicately scrubbing pale washes off tiny pans of color. He *has* to dig in and pick up a full brush loaded with pigment.

Paint Boxes, Palettes, and Colors

For some reason it is the tendency of most beginners to be afraid of pushing out the color from the tubes. I must confess I have enjoyed changing their habits in this regard, and on seeing a student squeeze out a pinhead size squirt of costly cobalt violet, I sometimes will say:

"It might be useful to have a little color on the palette to work with."

And with a delicate but firm squash I empty the tube into his box, where at least it stands a chance of being of some value.

When you reach the happy stage of first filling the new paintbox, and the colors lie pure and freshly coiled in their compartments, be careful not to tilt it until the colors set themselves. I generally place the newly replenished box in the sun for an hour or so until the colors stiffen and harden. I have seen a shambles of liquid colors all running into each other because this had not been done.

Assuming that we have obtained our color box and are ready to fill it, let us look over some of the many pigments which are the basic notes with which we do our composing. This list, naturally, as a personal matter of choice and varies with every watercolor painter. The list given here is a more or less standard one and I have suggested a group of useful colors which may be considered as additions to the regular palette of colors carried in the box. It is wise to experiment with these and if they are found of value to your particular way of working, they should be added to the box as a *must*.

It is useful, when setting out the colors in their compartments, to decide on some order of relationship. I like to keep all my blues next to

each other, then the greens, following down the line with yellows, reds, and finally the browns and umbers. In this way time is saved when reaching for a modulating color closely related in hue. The choice or arrangement is, of course, up to you, but it is a wise thing to know where your colors are so that you can automatically take a dab at the right spot without a second thought.

The list given presumes that the colors have been bought from a reliable firm whose products are consistently of a fine quality. It is interesting to note the differences which occur in standard makers' products. For years I have always had to add a tube of burnt sienna of a different brand from the rest of my colors. For some reason it has a *bite* and mixes better than other brands.

Let me remind you that watercolor, in essence, is nothing more than powdered colors derived from various sources—vegetable, animal, synthetic—bound into a workable form by the addition of binders—gum arabic, glycerine, etc. Diluted with water we are able to wash over our paper these various minerals and inert matter. Most reputable companies of today give us standardized colors and provide charts informing us of their permanency, covering power, etc. It may not seem important to us when we are beginning, but it is a good idea to insist on working with colors which will not suddenly fade from the page in a year or so. After all, one of these days we may do something we want to keep, and the fact that we have painted it in cheap and impermanent pigments will not please us. Good paper, good pigments—these should be a *must* from the start.

Here then, is the list. Those marked with a * are essential.

*ULTRAMARINE BLUE   One of the essential permanent colors. A good mixer, transparent, and found on most watercolor palettes.

*COBALT BLUE   A more opaque blue if used to full saturation. Diluted, it is an important color which is used for skies; mixed with pigments such as light red, raw sienna, or alizarin crimson it has a tendency to *granulate* or break into a diffused two-hued vibrating color which can be used to give liveliness to a passage. (See color reproduction in plate on techniques) page 74.

CERULEAN BLUE   A semi-opaque color, especially useful in skies. Tinted with a touch of cold yellow or cooled with a touch of viridian green it provides a cold robin's-egg blue which is impossible to imitate with other color mixtures. Used to full saturation it is dully opaque.

THALO BLUE (phthalocyanine)   A dark, staining blue which must be handled with care. Similar to a Prussian blue. Useful in providing very dark notes. As with all thalo colors, it must be used with discretion. Windsor blue is a similar strong dark blue.

*VIRIDIAN GREEN   A transparent green which makes a good basic mixer. Warmed with yellows or cooled with blues it provides a mid-green which can be modulated to the artist's desire.

HOOKER'S GREEN   There are many variations of this green, from the warm olive variety to the colder darker versions. I do not keep this on my regular palette, but it is a favorite of many landscape painters.

THALO GREEN (phthalocyanine)   An intense staining green which is useful when it can be handled properly. Otherwise it will stain and over-color a watercolor, giving it a cheap and bilious look. Useful for full intensity of darks.

There are many other versions of ready-mixed greens but as this is one of the most difficult colors to handle in watercolor, I have found the discipline of mixing greens from other colors very much worthwhile. Some of the richest subtle greens will be made from combinations of yellow, black, umber and a touch of blue. Others with burnt sienna and blue with a touch of the basic viridian. It is important to try all the various kinds on the market: cobalt green, emerald green, etc. Most artists avoid these colors, but you may find your favorite among them.

*YELLOWS   Here again the choice is more than ample. I like to have a cold primrose-type of yellow, a warm yellow and at times an almost orange type. The cadmiums serve this purpose for us: cadmium yellow light, deep, and cadmium orange. There are countless other types—staining yellows such as gamboge, the rare Indian yellow, the true variety of which has a strange origin. It seems that it is produced by extracting the dye from the urine of the camel after it has been induced to eat certain leaves, supposedly a very painful, if exotic process.

*YELLOW OCHRE   One of the subdued yellows, Like most of the yellows, very opaque and most useful when diluted with plenty of water.

*RAW SIENNA   A must with me, though for years I painted without it. Has a rich quality which is indispensable for foregrounds and modifying blues to neutral hue.

*ALIZARIN CRIMSON   A transparent rosy red which is found on most palettes. For mixing violets (with blues). For warming up skies—the slightest touch with the brush will pick up more than enough. Insidious when used inexpertly, it will dye and color the paper and is responsible for the garish look which many beginners have in their work.

ROSE MADDER   A lovely hue of crimson. Not included in the permanent colors in the box. The real madder, made from the madder root, is expensive and most makes are synthetic.

*CADMIUM RED   In its lightest hue resembles a vermilion. There are several darker cadmium reds, but the brilliant light-type makes a good base color. Very opaque when used undiluted, it is invaluable for warming up underwashes with ochre for a light, sunny glow on sunlit earth, foregrounds, etc. Used in small touches for a note of bright red, but with discretion.

*UMBER   Burnt and raw umber—two rich, subdued browns which mix beautifully with the ultramarines to give neutral grays so often used in stormy skies.

*PAYNES (also PAINES) GRAY   A rich blue-black which is also a sky *must*. This will often take the place of the Ivory or other blacks which are dangerous for most beginners as they have a way of dirtying up the other colors.

*LIGHT OR VENETIAN RED   Sometimes called English Red. I have a liking for this red which is most useful for warming grays. Indian red is a cooler, more opaque variety.

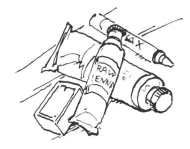

COBALT VIOLET   An opaque and rather sweet-looking violet which is not a good mixer, but fine effects can be made with it when used with cerulean or cobalt blue for skies of delicate tint.

COBALT GREEN   Also opaque. Somewhat similar to the more fugitive Emerald Green.

MARS RED, MARS YELLOW, ORANGE AND VIOLET   A group of iron oxide colors which are preferred by some. I see little advantage in them, but they are worth trying.

MANGANESE BLUE, VIOLET   Deep rich colors. I prefer the thalo or monastral blues.

SEPIA   Made from cuttlefish "ink," it is a useful color for making tonal wash drawings and combined with brown inks will give your sketches that "Old Master" look.

*LAMP BLACK, IVORY BLACK   Invaluable for making pen and wash studies similar to those shown on Page 93.

There are many other colors which painters like on their palettes. A few of these are listed here. Perhaps one of your favorites will be found here in preference to the choice above.

Brushes

In a recent catalog of artists' materials I found sixty-nine pages devoted to brushes alone, each page a closely packed list of sizes, types and some rather frightening prices. Not all of these were watercolor brushes, but most of them could be used for this purpose. Out of this wide choice we have to make our selection of one of the most important items of our equipment; a personal choice which can only be settled after we have tried a number of them.

As in the case of colors, I can only list here the

set of brushes which have become my favorites, plus a suggestion or two of other kinds which may appeal to you. Whatever you decide, *do not skimp on brushes.* Dig deep in your purse and pay out what will surely seem an unreasonable and outrageous price. Actually, this is not true. A good brush made from a fine, selected sable hair, constructed with years of experience behind it, is worth its weight in gold. During the war, when brushes and other materials became scarce, many of us would have paid any price to get decent, workable gear. I was fortunate in having a priority through my work as war artist overseas for the Canadian Navy, and could walk into the art stores in London and take my pick. Fortunately this problem of restricted material is no longer ours.

The paintings and charts in this book were painted with my usual sketching brushes, listed below.

No. 1 is a very special brush. I have had it since 1942 when I purchased it on my Navy art bill and the price must have been a shock to my commanding officer. By now the number has worn off, but I think it was the king of brushes. It was made from a selected super-long Russian red sable which is no longer obtainable. I think it was a number thirty. The makers catalog now lists as its highest, number 12, at twenty-two dollars. I asked them what it would cost to duplicate my brush and received the reply that it would be around one hundred dollars *if* they could obtain the hair! I have painted literally thousands of papers with this, and even now, though the brush does not come to the fine point it once did, it holds its spring and has plenty of life left in it. But you'll not need such an expensive item. You must, however, acquire one large red sable for a general working tool to put on large washes, and to handle the bold attack you are going to make on large sheets of paper when you do an important watercolor for an exhibition. It should be No. 9 or 10 at least and will cost you ten or eleven dollars. It will last for years if washed out with mild soap and brought to a point before being put away.

In addition, I have found the following four brushes essential to my painting kit: No. 2 or 3, a smaller edition of No. 9 or 10. Useful for linear work, picking out a detail, and drawing over the large washes.

Any one of several Japanese and Chinese brushes set in bamboo. These have a special type of stroke which I like for handling foliage. They are very cheap and though they do not last as long as a more expensive brush, are useful to have in the sketching outfit. The larger sizes are inclined to be soft and floppy and I buy only Nos. 1, 2 and 3.

A flat lettering brush. This need not be red sable, though this is preferable. A half-inch or three-quarter inch width is very useful. For covering large areas of sky with fast washes, it is indispensable.

No. 5 or 6. A ¾″ white bristle oil brush — flat, square ended. Useful for dry-brush scrubbing. You may have to cut the handle down to fit your brush case or paint box.

With these five basic brushes it should be possible to tackle any of the ordinary problems which you will come upon. In time, you will arrive at your own personal choice. Perhaps you will take a liking to the Chinese brush and use nothing else; or find you can handle a quick sketch completely with the one large sable. Whatever you do, don't try and paint a juicy, fresh watercolor with a tiny, three-haired brush. Test the brush when you buy it; even the best manufacturers turn out faulty products occasionally. Ask the art-dealer for some water and dip the brush in. Flip it free from water and see that it snaps back to a point and doesn't splay out. Try two or three until you are satisfied that it—your brush—is the best of the lot.

The felt-nib pen is a popular sketching instrument of recent invention. Though not actually a brush — it uses a felt nib which is controlled by pressing down on a valve in the pen to control the flow of ink — it has many advantages for rapid sketching. It dries instantly; thin, thick or brush-like lines can be made with it, and by taking out the nib from the pen and using it flat like a piece of crayon, charcoal-like tones can be made. Its one great fault to date; is that its inks fade. I have made test strips with the special inks for the various makes and have seen lines disappear completely when left in the strong sun for a week. For sketchbooks and nonpermanent work they are ideal. As you cannot rub out its lines, drawing with these pens is splendid training, for you must think before you put down your pen strokes. I find a half and half mixture of the black ink (which is slightly purple) and brown makes a rich sepia color.

Sketching Equipment

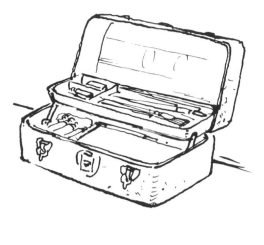

A most practical carrier for all. your gear is an ordinary fisherman's tackle box which, when open, has a secondary shelf with divisions. Buy a light, convenient-sized box which will hold your paint box, brushes and other needs. Mine even holds an army canteen of water with a cup fitted over it. It is also strong enough to be used as an emergency sketching stool. In a well-equipped outfit we will include the items listed below:

Watercolor box
Paint-rags, paper tissues, a small sponge
Pencil and erasers
White wax crayon
Thumb-tacks and one-edged razor blades
Felt-nib pen
Black India ink and pen
Bamboo or quill pens
Charcoal sticks
Extra tubes of colors
Brushes
Water canteen and cup

For my casein sketching box I use another tackle box. It carries my tubes of color, brushes, palette knife, and a folding tin palette which fits into the lid.

With this outfit, plus a light watercolor sketching easel you can start out on your sketching confident that you are well prepared. Always check your equipment before you leave. Discovering that you have left all your brushes at home is quite a shock; I've had it happen—several times!

Sketch Books

There has been much mention of sketchbooks in this book. Any convenient-sized strongly backed book is suitable. An all-around thin paper which will take pen and ink, felt-nib pen, and even, when wanted, a free wash or two, is the best. The spiral-bound variety is a very popular kind, but as you will, it is hoped, fill many of these notebooks, you'll have plenty of chance to try all kinds until you finally settle on the one you like.

I have on the shelf before me ten thick well-bound books containing two hundred pages each. They were made by a local bookbinder for me and I had him put in a variety of different thin papers which are favorites of mine. Saving discarded scraps of various papers, both white and tinted and gathering them into pages for a spring-back hard-cover book is another way of making your own sketchbooks with your own choice of assorted papers. They will provide a repository of ideas and keep a record of places, ideas and details of sketching trips. Long after I have sold the paintings made in some spot, I have thousands of drawings and scribbles which provide compositions for me continually.

The Qualities of Various Papers

It is essential that you learn the various qualities of the papers on which you paint, for paper plays a considerable role in watercolor. You can do this by finding out the hard way, ruining many sheets of paper, or by systematically testing and experimenting with the countless brands and types in the art stores.

Sooner or later you will discover your favorite kind and will develop your own preference for weight, comparative smoothness or rough texture. This choice will depend on the technique most personally suited to what you are trying to say.

Another important consideration, especially for the young student, is the cost of papers. During the depression years I learned more about papers during a year in France and Spain than in all the years since. The problem was to find a good, permanent nonfading paper at the cheapest price available. Unable to afford heavy handmade papers (or watercolor paints, for that matter) several of us did pen and wash drawings with two colored bottles of ink—blue and brown—on a semi-rag machine-made paper we found in a stationery store selling at a few cents for a huge sheet. I have some of these drawings still looking as fresh and unfaded as the day they were drawn.

Apart from economic reasons, the painter is being forced to try new papers all the time. Shipments of fine, handmade papers from England are scarce at times, Italian papers seem to vary in the amount of sizing on their surfaces, and new, fine papers appear on the market constantly. A recent American Watercolor Society paper competes favorably with the best English papers.

Certainly you will be able to paint excellent pictures on a fading, cheap, poor-surface paper. The chances are that it would have been an even better picture on good paper. You need not spend three dollars a sheet for the super-heavy, double-elephant, 400 pound, full-rag, handmade paper, but neither should you fight your washes onto a dull, unsympathetic, mechanical-textured paper which has you half-defeated before you begin.

Illustrated on page 95 are seven papers. It is important that you study what happens to the color and brush stroke on the individual sections of paper. The same color was used right across the page, and all conditions, such as amount of water and intensity of color, were kept as similar as possible. You can see for yourself what happens, even in the reduced size of the reproduction. The smooth paper rejects some of the color, absorbent papers such as Grumbacher "Aquarelle" seem to soak the color into the surface of the paper, darkening the value considerably. The Strathmore Student paper has a stamped-out texture which is irritating to anyone who has enjoyed better-grade paper. Handmade papers have the interesting irregularity of surface which is appealing in itself.

D'Arches, a fine French paper, is slightly creamier in color than the intense, brilliant white of Whatman, and comes in many different textures. Sometimes it has a tendency to dull the colors, perhaps because of a heavy "size" which should be washed off with clean water after stretching the paper.

Fabriano is an Italian paper and a favorite of

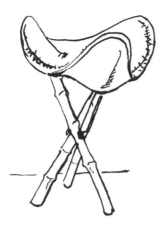

many, though not as crisp as Whatman. It is not included in the test-strip.

The last two on the test strip illustration are off-white examples which have their uses and followers. David Cox, sometimes available in large art supply houses, is a curious "oatmeal" textured and tinted paper which has the distinction of being named after its inventor-painter, an early English watercolor painter. It has a way of unifying colors, giving an all-over harmony.

Stretching Paper

This is a simple but annoying operation if it isn't done properly. Badly stretched, the paper can split or buckle. The procedure I use always seems to work and takes very little time.

Dampen the paper evenly with a sponge; it is not necessary to soak it. Have suitable length strips of brown gummed tape wet and ready to apply. Place the paper down rapidly on a drawing board. Smooth out bubbles or air pockets. Place the tape on the top edge of the paper and stick it

Monterey Boats (page 94) and Studio Interior (page 66) were painted on this paper.

Charcoal papers—Michelet, Ingres and lesser known names—provide a wide range of tinted surfaces worth trying. They are thin papers, and should either be mounted first on boards or stretched carefully, without too much dampening, lest they split when drying. They will not stand over-working or scrubbing, and the touch should be light and direct. Any use of the razor blade is prohibited. Japanese rice-paper has a special appeal and is also very fragile.

The question of weight is important. I like to use prestretched pads of paper of at least 140 lbs. A good sketching size is 14″ x 20″; for larger pictures 24″ x 30″ and 20″ x 24″. I prefer the 200 and 300 lb. papers for larger watercolors and always stretch them on a drawing board to prevent buckling while wet.

Notice how the color "breaks" its strokes on the rough papers, and how it flattens out on the smoother paper. This will determine the kind of "sparkle" you get to your washes.

Most painters use the best papers available. The sooner you learn to overcome the inhibiting fear of spoiling pristine sheets of expensive white paper, the sooner you'll be a watercolor painter. Those first touches will always be, I assure you, even after years of working, a bit like jumping into ice-cold water.

firmly to the board. If it needs firmer adhesion, place a thumbtack or two in the corners. Finish the other sides; add tape, tack and leave to dry. If you have worked deftly, the paper will stretch out as tight as a drum in an hour or so. It will also lie flat even when cut from the board after the painting is finished. You may have trouble with this seemingly simple task—I have seen students get themselves in quite a flurry over it. But after a few tries, it will be easier.

Additional Equipment for Casein Painting

A flat white-enamelled butcher's tray makes a practical and easily cleaned palette for casein painting. Be sure to wash it off after each painting session, as in a few days the paint can dry as hard as a rock.

Save your old brushes, both oil and watercolor, for use in scrubbing-in casein. Be sure to wash them thoroughly with soap and water after the day's work.

A palette knife, scrapers, razor blades are useful tools for scratching down to underpainting through wet or dry pigment. Sometimes the end of the brush handle is useful to make textured furrows in the wet paint. A photographer's hard rubber roller, four or six inches wide, is a handy tool for rolling on textures for a broken ground on which to paint. Sponges and plenty of paint rags are invaluable.

The number of pigments you use should be limited at first until you get the "feel" of the casein. Start with a few primary colors, a blue, red and yellow, along with black and white. Gradually add the earth colors, the ochres, siennas, etc. A limited palette of venetian red, black, blue and white will give you plenty of scope for simple color schemes. Shiva lists thirty-one colors on its color card. From these you can build up your own favorite palette. I use a similar list of colors to that marked with a star in the watercolor list. You may find the brand names confusing—Ponsol blue, Shiva blue, etc., but a comparison of the color card with the more familiar names will soon clarify this. Changing the water jar constantly is essential as the opaque pigment soon sullies the water. For your first efforts use a fairly heavy paper with some texture to it. Heavy illustration board or 300 pound watercolor paper is best for larger paintings.

Some of the additional materials you may use are listed below. Most manufacturers of casein have their own recommendations for the use of the products they make. It is wise to use the pigments and varnishes of one brand to obtain a consistency of working method. I have preferred Shiva colors for their covering power, their resistance to drying up in the tube and for their similarity of mixing qualities, though there are many other fine brands on the market. A tube of casein will occasionally go hard and once dried-up must be discarded—another reason for working

with it steadily instead of storing it on the shelf.

Shiva Ethereal Varnish: A sweet-smelling varnish which is used to bring up the darks when they dry too mat and light in value. Should be brushed or sprayed on very lightly over the casein when dry. (A built-up, saturated surface of many coats of casein will naturally take longer to dry than a one-coat brushing. Allow two or three hours at least, before varnishing.) The varnish dries with a semi-gloss. If shiny spots show, apply another thin coating. This varnish will isolate the casein before applying watercolor glazes.

Shiva Emulsion: A milky liquid used for thinning out the casein pigment. It is not necessary to use this, and I seldom do. If you like the consistency of water, emulsion and pigment, be sure that the emulsion does not exceed one part of emulsion to five parts of water or the colors will become foggy or milky.

Glazing Varnish: A varnish which is used with oil paint to thin down the colors to apply transparent layers of color over casein underpainting. For varnishing the final picture to convert a casein into an oil-like finish, Shiva recommends a very thin coat of Ethereal varnish first; after two hours a coat of Glazing varnish, later (two or three days) a second coat of Glazing varnish. If spotty, a third coat may be applied, after an interval of several days.

Shiva Media: Used as a retouch varnish and as a thinner for oil colors, using one part of Shiva Media to four parts of turpentine.

BEING YOUR OWN CRITIC

"What is wrong?" So often in an art class the picture is presented to the instructor for criticism with this question tossed after it. The wise instructor, accustomed to his job, looks worriedly at the picture for a moment, smiles, and tosses the question right back: "What do *you* think is wrong with it."

Learning to make a critical diagnosis of your work is not an easy thing to do. It requires knowledge and experience along with the particular sense of intuition of the "rightness" of a color and form which is the mainspring of your picture-making in the beginning. Nevertheless, after you have done your best and still know that something is lacking somewhere but cannot put your finger on it, the careful consideration and analysis of your work by a more experienced painter may be of value to you.

If you have really studied this book and painted steadily while doing so, you will be much better equipped than you were before to be a critic of your own work. A check list, even though abstracting and oversimplifying the process of diagnosis, might be of value to you here. Perhaps one of these suggestions may be the root of your trouble. The probability is that your work is lacking only to a degree here and there in many of these positive qualities which are listed below.

What was your real interest, your basic concept, your dominant mood? As interpretation, is it fresh and penetrating, or does it consist of borrowed and superficial forms? Is it honestly yours, giving meaning to your intuitions and personal feelings, or is it an echo of someone else's pictures? Have you made something new, or are you still trying to compete with the color camera? Is the picture technically good but empty of feeling? Or does it try to say something too far beyond your present technical skills?

Assuming a valid and pictorial interest on your part, how well does the structure explore and deliver it? How about the organization of linear movement on the surface and the considerations of objects placed in pictorial space? Is there a dominant note and lesser repetitions of it, one main theme with lesser ornamentation? Have you been able to throw all these design "rules" out the window and still make your picture vitally alive and whole?

How is your feeling for forms, basic and developed; the quality of your line drawing? Do your tonal patterns work together, subtly interwoven and persuasive, your textural feeling attract or repel? Where are the distracting elements, the dead areas which do not function? Whatever the tensions and contrasts within, does the picture as a unit have the orchestrated impact and convincing "wholeness" of a work of art?

And distortions? Are they genuine, the changes of perspective and anatomy contributing to your expression, based on knowledge and emotion, and not on a whim or ignorance? Has the structure of your object been understood and interpreted through its rightful form? Are your symbols borrowed tricks—useful or not—or freshly conceived? Is your drawing timid, niggling or bold, free and effective for your purpose?

Have you explored the possibilities and respected the limitations of your medium? Are you trying to make it look like something else? Is your brush work contrived, tricky or merely craftsmanship-like? Have you used your own color sense to the fullest extent, do the colors work for you to help express the feelings you are painting?

When you have found a muddled concept, or a composition that falls to pieces, or dirty, discordant colors, your diagnosis may be quick and to the point. But as you improve and the reasons for your failures begin to evade you, your self-criticism may move into other fields. Then you may find it helpful to consider the quality of your imagination, and the basic strengths or weaknesses of your mind as a painter. In these very difficult and subjective matters, any check list such as this one would be of even more question-

able value. Perhaps the thing to do at this stage is to read more and better books and listen to good music.

One helpful habit is that of hanging your work on your own walls and studying it for weeks and months. Often when you least expect it, a glance at the right time will give the clue to what is lacking. Another way is just the opposite—that of putting your work away for a long time and then looking at it with a fresh eye. Often, after a time, the remedy for what seemed to have been a lost cause will seem obvious.

Whatever happens, you will have the satisfaction of having been your own jury. At times you may be appalled by what you see. Occasionally you will gaze with wonderment and awe, asking yourself: "Did *I* do that?" And hoping that sometime you will be able to do it again.

SHOWING YOUR WORK

When you have reached the point where you feel that your work is getting good enough to send into local or amateur contests and exhibitions, you will come up against the problem of deciding what is your best. What should you choose to represent you? You look through your portfolios trying desperately to decide what is worth mounting and framing. After you have been your own critic you will have eliminated many, leaving yourself perhaps half a dozen of the best to choose from.

Unlike the oil painter, you will have amassed a large body of work in a short time. If you have kept at it steadily for a year—even doing two watercolors or caseins a week—you will have accumulated a pile of over a hundred papers. How many of these are worth saving? How can you eliminate and throw aside the worthless papers which are definitely failures, perhaps using the backs of them for other efforts?

This is the time to invite an artist-friend to help you. Get him to go over your collection with you. The chances are that he will see value in many of your things which you are ready to scrap. But don't believe *everything* he says—artists are notably inclined to let their own likings and prejudices influence and color their judgments. Take the precaution of asking someone to look at your efforts who is sympathetic to the idiom in which you work. You will only be discouraged and invite disaster to ask a rabid academician to look at your abstract efforts, or—if you are a realist—a nonobjective enthusiast to look at your studies from nature. Counter the professional criticism you receive with a showing of your work to intelligent persons who are not professional painters, but who have a love and understanding of paintings. They, in the final analysis, are the *real* jury. Balance their reactions with the artist's, and you may be able to help your own final decision . . . "This is what I will send to the exhibition, or frame to hang on my own wall."

Whatever you do, do not destroy your work too quickly. Put it away. Look at it a long time later to see what kind of progress you are making. Old sketches, when seen anew, often serve as ideas for new pictures and compositions, and many times will act as reference sheets for color schemes with new subjects. On the other hand, don't take yourself so seriously that, after several years of hard work, you feel that you have arrived and cannot understand why your pictures are not suddenly snatched from you at fabulous prices or sought by purchasing committees.

Experiment constantly. Try all the ways suggested in this book and in others. And remember that what and how you paint is, in finality, your choice. Put it all down in *your* way so that your personal vision will not come from the eye alone, but from the demands and pressures of your own inner self.

Good painting!

BIBLIOGRAPHY OF USEFUL BOOKS

ART STUDENT'S ANATOMY
  by Edmond J. Farris
  J. B. Lippincott Co.

ART AND VISUAL PERCEPTION
  by Rudolf Arnheim
  Faber

ARTISTS ON ART, FROM XIV TO THE XX CENTURY
  Compiled and edited by Robert
  Goldwater and Marco Treves
  Pantheon Books

CEZANNE'S COMPOSITION
  Analysis of His Form with
  Diagrams and Photographs.
  by Erle Loran
  University of California Press

CREATIVE PERSPECTIVE
  by Ernest W. Watson
  Reinhold Publishing Corp.

ELEMENTARY PRINCIPLES OF LANDSCAPE PAINTING
  by John F. Carlson
  Sterling Publishing Co.

ENJOYING MODERN ART
  by Sarah Newmeyer
  Reinhold Publishing Corp.

DRAWING TREES
  by Henry C. Pitz
  Watson-Guptill Publications

HOW PAINTINGS HAPPEN
  by Ray Bethers
  W. W. Norton & Co.

JOHN MARIN
  by Mackinley Helm
  Pellegrini & Cudahy, in association
  with the Institute of Contemporary
  Art, Boston

ON THE LAWS OF JAPANESE PAINTING
  by Henry P. Bowie
  Dover Books

PERSPECTIVE DRAWING, FREEHAND AND MECHANICAL
  by Joseph W. Hull
  University of California Press

THE ART OF THE ARTIST
  Theories and techniques of art
  by the artists themselves.
  Compiled by Arthur Zaidenberg
  Crown Publishers Inc.

THE NAKED TRUTH AND PERSONAL VISION
  by Bartlett H. Hayes, Jr.
  Addison Gallery of American Art

THE NATURAL WAY TO DRAW
  by Kimon Nicolaides
  Houghton & Mifflin

TREATISE ON LANDSCAPE PAINTING
  by Andre Lhote

TREES AND LANDSCAPES
  by Ted Kautzky
  Reinhold Publishing Corp.

DATE DUE

SEP 5 90			
GAYLORD			PRINTED IN U.S.A.